In Search of God

In Search of God
From Definition to Discovery and Quest

J. Gregory Steiner

Copyright © 2022 J. Gregory Steiner.

All rights reserved. No part of this book may be used or reproduced by any means, graphic, electronic, or mechanical, including photocopying, recording, taping or by any information storage retrieval system without the written permission of the author except in the case of brief quotations embodied in critical articles and reviews.

Archway Publishing books may be ordered through booksellers or by contacting:

Archway Publishing
1663 Liberty Drive
Bloomington, IN 47403
www.archwaypublishing.com
844-669-3957

Because of the dynamic nature of the Internet, any web addresses or links contained in this book may have changed since publication and may no longer be valid. The views expressed in this work are solely those of the author and do not necessarily reflect the views of the publisher, and the publisher hereby disclaims any responsibility for them.

Any people depicted in stock imagery provided by Getty Images are models, and such images are being used for illustrative purposes only. Certain stock imagery © Getty Images.

Scripture quotations marked (JB) are taken from the JERUSALEM BIBLE Copyright© 1966, 1967, 1968 by Darton, Longmand & Todd LTD and Doubleday and Co. Inc. All rights reserved.

Scripture quotations marked (GNT) are from the Good News Translation in Today's English Version- Second Edition Copyright © 1992 by American Bible Society. Used by Permission.

ISBN: 978-1-6657-2441-8 (sc)
ISBN: 978-1-6657-2440-1 (hc)
ISBN: 978-1-6657-2442-5 (e)

Library of Congress Control Number: 2022909911

Print information available on the last page.

Archway Publishing rev. date: 06/24/2022

To the memory of St. Paul, who brilliantly shared the defining moments of his Jewish faith, allowing his discovery of Christ to permeate the inquiring minds of his time, while humbly preaching humankind's need for continuing its quest for fulfillment.

Contents

Introduction xi

1. Clarifying Important Terms: What Are We
   Talking About? 1
   Definition 2
   Discovery 4
   Quest for Fulfillment 6
2. Is Happiness Just Another Term? It Is Much More. 9
   Happiness Is beyond Definition 10
   What Is Spiritual Happiness? 14
3. Is Our Initial Contact with God Satisfying?
   Probably Not. 19
   The Searching for God Conundrum 20
   Our Parental God 24
   The Judaic and Christian Vision of God 27
4. Can We Talk about Creation and Eternity in
   Our Search for God? Why Not? 33
   Old and New Paradigms 35
   The Traditional Paradigm 35
   The Spiritual Creation Wheel 37
   Beginnings and Endings 42
5. Are Divine Revelation and Inspiration God-
   Given Truths? Yes and No. 45
   Consequences for Revelation and Inspiration 48
   What Are the Revelations behind Inspired
   Biblical Stories? 50
6. Are Myths and Mysterious Revelations True?
   Not as We Have Traditionally Believed. 54

How Is Original Sin a Myth? 56
　　　Understanding God Is Not How We Experience God..... 59
　　　Discovering the Qualities of God 62
7.　Are Our Early Ideas about Divinity and Jesus
　　Beneficial for Us? Yes, but Newer Ideas Are Needed......... 66
　　　A Starting Point on Divinity.. 67
　　　Humanity versus Divinity... 71
　　　Old Testament Understanding of Divinity 71
　　　What Is Meant by the Son of God? 75
8.　Are There Other Religions That Offer Eternal
　　Salvation? Yes... 83
　　　Circumcision and Defining a Religion 88
　　　Death to All outside a Covenant Relationship.................. 90
　　　No Salvation outside a Covenant Relationship 91
　　　What Salvation in Other Religions Could Mean 93
9.　Can Any Discovery about God Allow Us to
　　Continue Our Search? It Should...................................... 100
　　　Taking Another Look at the Necessary
　　　Qualities of a God..101
　　　Reality versus the Eucharistic Presence 104
　　　Survival of the Soul... 108
10.　Are There Other Ways of Understanding
　　 Eternity? Probably. 112
　　　God and Eternity for the Israelites and Early Christians 114
　　　An Experience of the Eternal Involves an
　　　Unfulfilled Quest for God 116
　　　A Continual Quest for God Fuels Happiness 120
　　　Why We Need to Continue the Quest for God.............. 121
　　　Eternity Is Not an Endpoint but a Journey 122
　　　The Adam and Eve Myth.. 123
　　　The Suffering Sacred Heart and the Immaculate Heart.... 124
　　　What Did Jesus Say about Eternity? 127
11.　Are We Creating Our Ideas about God? So What?........ 131
　　　Are God's Ways Our Ways? Probably Not 132

    Creating God's Will for Us 135
    The Need for Sacred Images in Prayer............................ 138
12. Is It Possible to Experience Eternity Now? Why Not? 142
    Mystics in Church History... 144
    Eternity as Experienced through the Kingdom of God...148
    Another Look at Jesus's Resurrection..............................149
    A Life with Loved Ones after Death.............................. 153
    What Others Think about Life Now versus Life
    after Death 156
13. Can We Find Eternal Meaning in Life? It Is
    Time to Start Looking. 161
    Primary Purpose in Life...161
    The Legacy of Victor Frankl... 163
    A Closer Look at Humankind's Search for
    Ultimate Meaning... 165
    A Final Note 169

Acknowledgments 173
Endnotes 175
Bibliography 179

Introduction

With the outbreak of COVID in Canada, most businesses and public ventures were in lockdown, resulting in some unusual and unforeseen consequences. These consequences were more than just the ordinary challenges of staying at home for months. Loss of jobs, school closures, and numerous COVID restrictions were also momentous. As an author, I had additional time for pondering my Christian faith. Perhaps, by using my time well, I could spend a few productive months writing an article or two for my own personal benefit. As it turned out, the epidemic became a pandemic, and what was expected to be only a few months of isolation became two years; what were to be only a few words turned out to be another manuscript.

In my initial work, *The Evolution of Belief*,[1] I specifically focused on the importance of always being ready, when discussing religious topics, to accept the possibility of new insights into our belief system. We find out in our senior years that wisdom comes from integrating important experiences in life. This wisdom can only become fruitful when it arises out of a discovery of something new and enlightening. It comes after our faith has incorporated a new insight about God and all of His creation—including humankind. This process is an ongoing one and lifelong in nature. My book is like a sequel to *The Evolution of Belief*, in that it offers you a look at belief but from a personal point of view. Given the acceptance and incorporation of the discoveries of science into our belief system, as outlined in my previous book, we can now move ahead as to how this bit of wisdom might express itself in our daily Christian lives.

I admit my life as a teacher has greatly influenced the way I write. You are encouraged to read my chapters only as an invitation and not look at the chapters as if there will be an examination on the selected subjects in the near future. In the process of sharing with you my insights, I also share many experiences that have come about in my personal and religious life. My personal life experiences serve as a vehicle for sharing important and insightful discoveries arrived at as my faith in God matured. Bear with me as I move through sensitive items of our traditional Christian belief. I am optimistic that you will resonate not only with many of my insights but with many of the personal and religious experiences that have occurred in my life as well.

My first book was a scientific analysis of the development of dogmas and doctrine over the stretch of Christianity's existence. This book, *In Search of God: From Definition to Discovery and Quest*, is more of a religious work, which hinges on my personal experience with religious concepts arrived at throughout my life. My experience of a deity now is not the same as in my younger years, or even in many years of my adult life. I have discovered that, if there is value to my experience of religion, it is a value that urges me to look forward and not be satisfied with a given belief or doctrine for personal fulfillment.

As in my first work, where I mentioned the importance of treasuring past religious traditions as valuable contributions to our faith, so also, in this work, I wish to make it clear that I am not disparaging Christians' insistence on being totally satisfied with the status quo regarding their items of beliefs. However, I have taught in high schools, and my teaching habits persist throughout my life. So I ask that you be patient and know my intent is to share, not to impose my ideas on you. I have always defined, discovered, and will always continue on my quest for more enlightenment. In

Sc. + Spirituality

this work, I wish to show how, in today's world, we are invited to look forward to a new religious experience of God that falls in line with what we know about the world and a new world view that includes God.

It is easy to discuss, on a philosophical and theological level, the need to change our ideas about creation, incarnation, and redemption in today's world. However, it is quite a challenge to deal with these needs from a kneeling position in a church pew. It would be much easier to let such insights slide away and keep them to ourselves, which would be unfortunate. This work will respond to that slip-and-slide tendency.

My intent in this work is to show how we can express to our Christian friends some new ideas without causing them to disown us as true Christian believers. How can I talk about doctrines and dogmas of belief in a new way without being an outcast, an outlier? How can I approach the believing community when opening scripture to share something different about a divine message? The following chapters will attempt to show how I can achieve this. If taken to heart, my book may provoke surprise and an admission that faith needs to move in a new direction for people who are searching for God in their lives.

Although our understanding of maturity is straightforward with regard to behavior in family and society, the progression of maturity in matters of religious belief is not as easily understood. In fact, it is often the case that attitudes with entrenched beliefs have little or no tolerance for new insights and understanding. For example, a person with a literal interpretation of Genesis may respond to the big bang theory with the following complaint: "What do you mean the world was not created in seven days?" We can continue to celebrate key religious events and ceremonies in a Christian community, but there must be a continual evolution of those events and ceremonies. It is similar to the fact that Santa Claus and the Easter Bunny cannot possibly mean the same thing for adults as they do for children. From a religious point of view, an adult understanding and appreciation of Christmas and Easter should never be limited to the insights that a child or adolescent experiences. It is not that these initial stories are incorrect or untrue experiences in our early years, but that a maturing faith should not hear these biblical stories repeatedly with the same meaning and understanding as that of children.

Theologians have suggested that maturity in religion can be somewhat suppressed when there is an entrenched idea of God given to us through divine revelation. This is because if any new perspectives of a belief are proposed, they are regarded as offensive to the original faith experience. However, if understandings of dogmas and doctrines of faith do not develop as we grow into adulthood and beyond, then our belief becomes stale and less meaningful for us as Christian believers. As the adolescent matures, the understanding of matters of faith should be allowed to mature as well. It is not that we disregard traditional beliefs, but rather we accept them for what they are: stepping-stones on our journey to a more adult faith experience of God.

The first six chapters concern themselves with what we mean by God from a historical point of view. Having proposed a position with carefully clarified terms, I initially discuss happiness and why it is important for a good faith experience. I treat different personal ideas about God and propose a new way of looking at creation and eternity. The relevance of revelation is discussed and what modern theology brings to the table about myths and mysterious revelations.

Chapters 7 and 8 treat the concepts of divinity, the Son of God, and how all religions may preach a path to eternity. Chapters 9 and 10 show how discovery always leads us to a further search about the qualities of God, and what eternity could mean when we are looking for a spiritual fulfillment. Chapter 11 treats the question of humankind creating our own ideas about God and how this could be the cause of continued quest for fulfillment in our lives. The Christian message is always shared within a given time context and always interpreted by certain institutions and cultures. Chapter 12 is an explanation of what eternity (even life after death) might possibly mean if the kingdom of God is present in us now. Chapter 13 attempts to show how finding ultimate meaning in life can be our introduction to eternity.

The pages of this book move through the subject matter in a way that the average believer can understand. I do not delve deeply into rationalism and ethical philosophy. Although I am also a biologist, this work does not relate to the basic tenets of a natural theology. I say that just as life continually evolves, so also my ideas about spirituality evolve. My ideas about God and related topics should never exhibit a static position. It follows then that my experience of the divine presence of God within me is evolving, as well. What this means is that I am constructing an idea of God that is continually changing, and with these new insights, I discover an increasing experience of God. This book will share with you how this happened in my life.

Our idea of God is a construct constantly being refashioned by our ongoing inquiry about a deity. Searching for God will be just that: always a quest with further questions and answers. A quest can lead us to realize a need to continually look for more discoveries about God. In my book, I propose that searching for a God should generate not only a positive religious attitude but also an ongoing journey filled with many episodes of happiness.

This work cannot and will not satisfy everyone, but it should cause us to stop and look at the way we view the deity we call our God. The thoughts expressed are controversial and perhaps upsetting to believers whose spiritual life fits solidly within a traditional perspective. Even so, the opportunity is there for us to experience a profound sense of freedom to explore a new way of looking at self-fulfillment and a new way of grasping the incomprehensible. What I offer is a new way to move forward on a constant journey we can call eternity. Enjoy the book.

1

Clarifying Important Terms: What Are We Talking About?

At some time in the past, we have all been victims of our own making. I have led or participated in discussions where I realized later that an impasse could have been averted had there been clarification of terms or ideas at the very beginning. However, when having a casual coffee with acquaintances, the last thing we think of is to start a conversation with a common understanding of terms. When discussing sensitive topics with friends, it is always important to be aware of the need to compromise and accommodate—or at least agree to disagree in order to preserve friendship.

Science and religion have always been hot topics for me. Controversies about science are relatively easy for me to resolve, but religious matters are different, since there is less likely to be common understanding for discussion. I enjoy talking about concepts and terms in the fields of science and religion. Terms relating to science are often more universal. Terms in religion are somewhat vague and can certainly be personal. Such circumstances could result in many impasses and failures in communication.

I remember from my days teaching biology that it was very important to do two things: (1) to make sure the students knew where I was going in a lecture by outlining my presentation for them; and (2) to make sure they understood the content by defining difficult terms that occurred in the lecture and on their assignment sheets. This approach also helped me stay focused and not get sidetracked. I have chosen to do the same thing in this book.

At the beginning, I want to share my understanding of some reoccurring concepts. I am inviting you to understand these terms in slightly different ways as you move through the chapters of this book. The words are *definition*, *discovery*, and *quest*, found in the title of this work. Although the connotations of these words may be rather new or change a bit through the chapters, it is important to have some starting point or initial common understanding of the words and concepts involved.

Definition

This word implies something to be identified, in which parameters have been drawn, with meanings to be shared and accepted by others. In a wider view, the word necessarily includes an array of contributions from a vast number of educated, erudite persons, with at least a universal acceptance and understanding of the word or topic. To define could also mean to finalize, in a finished fashion, something or someone as being this and not some other meaning, thing, or person. When discussing words and concepts like "God," "truth," "search," and "eternity," along with a host of other common words, there will undoubtedly be challenges, even at the best of times.

In my work, I treat definition with an enduring respect when discussing past traditions and truths about spiritual matters, especially in the treatment of our idea of God. In our youth, we were instructed about God in a definitive sense; that is, we were told that God is all good and not evil. Secondly, God is all knowing and not dependent on anyone or anything for understanding. Thirdly, God is all powerful and has no need to depend on anyone or anything to attain His wishes. These are our initial thoughts about God, and they are a mirror or reflection of our elders' thoughts and teachings. There are many other definitions of God we might discuss at the outset of this book, but all definitions, however many there are of God, are handed down to us as final—that is, teachings we were told are true beyond question and, for the most part, should not be challenged.

In most chapters of this book, I clearly and continually state that when searching for God in our lives, the act of defining continually stabilizes us in some sort of faith experience. This not only holds us to some truth about a deity, but it is also the only way we can communicate with others about items of our beliefs that are important for our faith. For example, when we say to someone, "God bless you" or "God be with you," we are assuming that He is always present to us in some way. Although the following chapters of this book use God and divine presence interchangeably, the two are not exactly the same. We all have our own ideas about God. But the words *divine presence* require a deeper sense of acknowledgment from us. Divine presence, unlike a defined idea of God, will carry a personal experience within and unique to the recipient.

Defining God is a constant tendency, regardless of our age or status as believers. As we grow in faith, we implicitly call to mind what it is that we believe. Defining our ideas of God, at any stage, becomes a framework for moving on to something a bit deeper and more experiential. This leads us to the second quality or characteristic of someone who is searching for God. This second stage is called discovery.

Discovery

This stage conveys a sense that something is now uncovered, as it were, for the first time. My understanding of *discovery* incorporates the following: coming across something you thought you understood in a definitive sense but now see as something new. Robert Schuller put it well when he said, "An explorer has truly discovered something when he has travelled across the whole world, and, coming back to where he first started, has seen the place for the first time."[2] Such an exploration does not include just that the idea or place is entirely new but also that it has been viewed from a different or maturing perspective.

In spirituality, when talking about God, a maturing mind should continually be experiencing something new about God. We should always be open to new insights about a divine presence among us. This phenomenon is called spiritual growth. I firmly believe that this is important for retaining an appreciation of the spiritual in our lives. However, there are challenges to this thinking. It implies that we need to be ready to move out of our comfort zone in religious matters. This is not easy, since we want to treasure the good things we have learned about God in our lives. Although good and noble, a discovery about God and His influence in our lives cannot be the final thought on the matter. In order to maintain spiritual growth in our lives, we need to continually explore our ideas about God.

In a true sense, when discovering God in our lives as a new experience, we must accept any definitive stage to be relative and not permanent. If we are not moving ahead with new discoveries about God as someone we see for the first time, then we simply do not move ahead in our search for God. Consequently, spiritual growth cannot occur—rather a steady-state condition persists that runs the risk of becoming stagnant, resulting in loss of religious fervor. As an example, let us use the concept of church and what it could mean for us. Initially, for me, the word meant a building with four sides, a roof, and steeple. Later on in my life, with the help of priests and nuns and teachers, the word now has a much deeper meaning—it is the people of God.

While the church is still a special building, set apart from any other kind of building, a new insight has been uncovered that tells me more about myself and the people of God. Acceptance and appreciation of something new enhances my faith and knowledge of God. The church as a structure is now personalized and made human for the first time. This was a real discovery for me.

Another moment of discovery happened with the concept of the creation. Once defined for us according to the book of Genesis, we experienced a steady state with no movement ahead. However, with what we now know about science's discoveries and knowledge about the origins of the universe, we must reflect and assert that the creation could not have been a seven-day series or feat. This discovery allows us to look at the same concept and see it as if it were new, or at least different. This could lead to a discovery not only about the creative act of God but something new about God Himself as well.

The idea that the Bible is the Word of God and should be taken only in a literal sense is questionable. This will lead us to another discovery. We now discover that God's Word is always couched in the context of the time. God's Word emanates out of the mouths of believers who experienced God in their own way thousands of years ago. Ancient understandings about God were always time sensitive and should always be respected and treasured as such. Contemporary beliefs are the same way. They are items of faith communicated in the here and now. Admittedly, this discovery is not accepted by many Christians, Jews, and Muslims.

All the chapters of this book will offer examples of instances in our lives that are definitive and discovery experiences. However, the last and third characteristic of belief is not common and will be most forceful and controversial. It is called the quest, which is what I propose is the drive for ultimate fulfillment.

Quest for Fulfillment

The most difficult idea to grasp is that discovery about spirituality can never be complete. Although a new discovery about God does enrich our lives, its effects are not permanent, and there is always that ongoing sense of wonder and incompletion with each discovery. There is a suspicion deep within that each new discovery is not all there is to learn about our new insight or spiritual experience. Our quest or desire for fulfillment in God, by its nature, should never convey a sense of finality. We cannot say, "We have found our pie in the sky," or "This is the way it is," or that "This pie in the sky will never change." In other words, we should never be satisfied with something new we have learned about a divine presence in our lives. This is a novel way of viewing fulfillment. To have such an unending quest for God in our lives can be disconcerting. We want to think of heaven as a spiritual goal or finality, of being with the eternal God as if enjoying a final resting place with God. I am saying this cannot be the case and will never occur when we are searching for an ultimate spirituality in our lives.

This third theme, which penetrates most of my thinking throughout this book, is the most difficult to accept. Why? It is because we are always searching for a final answer or view about God. We are always looking for finality or closure. My proposal in this book is that a quest for God is very much like a journey with no end; a spiritual happiness or fulfillment must be found in the journey itself and not equated with the satisfaction that I have actually possessed something securely. You may find this aspect of the quest difficult to accept, because it is not a good feeling to find out that what we are searching for will never be found or possessed in its totality. I ask you to be patient as I work through the following chapters with important items of belief, using the tools of definition, discovery, and quest for fulfillment.

In conclusion, I believe it is important that we first look at definition, discovery, and quest for a common understanding before delving into the next chapters. My intention is not to convince you of anything but to provide a series of recognizable signals about the way I approach an understanding of God. However, our personal relationship with a divine being is just that—personal. Those ideas that come up about God in community are relational and do rely upon a common understanding among those with whom we are connected in prayer and common religious worship.

The point of my book is to set the groundwork for a personal mindfulness about the presence of God in our lives. This experience is not something we need to define and defend to others. It just is, and like faith, we must always be maturing in that personal experience. The presence of God in our lives will never be exactly the same experience for everyone. Each of us is unique in our experience of God, and that is why God is so special to us. Furthermore, our quest for the divine presence of God cannot be reproduced in anyone else. It is unique and will always culminate in a special and unique drive for a continued fulfillment. Definition, leading to a discovery and further quest, is what fuels our faith in God. We hope and expect them to light our way to a new and greater appreciation of God in our lives.

2
Is Happiness Just Another Term? It Is Much More.

I initially thought the idea of happiness should be one of the last topics treated in this book. As I completed my ideas about the search for a God experience, I felt it adequate to first explore the difficult concepts about the first objective—that is, the search—without attempting to talk about the possibility that I might not be content and relatively satisfied with my search for God at the end of the line.

Having fully contemplated the matter, I realized that unless people are happy, what is the point of any quest or movement toward self-fulfillment. As I attempt to expand my search of God in detail, would I be able to say that I have experienced some level of contentment with my work here? Why would I convince myself to proceed with an approach to the idea of a search for God unless there was an experiential value attached? Unless I achieved a higher level of happiness and contentment in moving this way, there would be no lasting value to the *search* idea. Consequently, I chose happiness as the topic of my second chapter because of the need to set the stage, which is to say I needed to explain what spiritual contentment means, as opposed to other forms of satisfaction and contentment a person might experience in life. I am convinced that happiness, like any spiritual experience involving the discovery of God, may be similar but not the same as any other satisfying experience. I will explain this in detail, but now let us look at this subject of happiness.

Happiness Is beyond Definition

Happiness is a word much like love and life. However you try to put parameters around it, another valid point pops up, adding a new insight. We all have our unique experience of contentment and satisfaction with life. Yet all of us understand what happiness means. We can look at happiness as a form of contentment of the mind. At least it is more than just having bodily health or financial wealth, although these are often associated with happiness. Most people we know want happiness, and it is truly obvious when we come upon someone who is not happy.

Happiness assumes there is a sense of joy for what has been achieved, or pleasure in knowing that something in the future is under our control. Happiness on some level represents a modicum of fulfillment, and when it happens to us personally, it becomes a form of self-fulfillment. The ancients believed happiness could be arrived at through a withdrawal from desires, or at least controlling desires in our lives. This makes sense if we believe that the accumulation of goods is the objects of our desires. It would result in an unending quest for possessions, power, and control over others and would leave one unhappy, unfulfilled, or at least frustrated.

As a child, I felt content with myself and being with others, particularly those in my immediate family. Initially, I believed that toys, sweet foods, and funny movies played a major role in making me happy. However, if challenged, I would have admitted I also needed assurance, acceptance, and familial love to bring me contentment. As I grew older, the possession of worldly goods also appeared to be very important to me. Acquiring a new bicycle, my driver's license, and then a car of my own were highlights of my youth, bringing a deep sense of satisfaction and happiness. I was now assuming that those material objects offered acceptance, protection, and love. In my youth, I had no idea that I could not find real happiness in material belongings. To illustrate this idea, I would like to share a story told by a modern Indian guru:

> Once a man went to a saint by traveling far in the mountains. He asked the holy man, "Sir, I have a question which is bothering me. If you answer that I will give you 1000 gold coins which I am carrying in my purse." He asked, "What is happiness? Please make me understand." The saint was silent for a while and then grabbed the purse and ran. The man stood aghast and started chasing him. After running for a while, the saint stopped and sat under a tree. The man ran up to him and grabbed his purse back. There was an instance of joy on his face, which brightened on retrieving his purse. He asked the saint what was wrong with him and why did he do so.
>
> To which the saint smiled and answered, "What you felt the instant when you got back your purse is what happiness is."
>
> Earlier the bag was with him, but it did not keep him happy. But when he lost it, instantly his mind programmed that only if he receives his purse will he be happy.

You have programmed your mind into a computer logic wherein if you get this you will be happy, else you are not. You created this definition (happiness) yourself, and nobody is responsible for it.

If I get 90% marks, then I will be happy. Else, I will be unhappy.

However, the programming logic is much more complex as you keep updating with "if" and "else" conditional loops. You are stuck in your own infinite loop and keep losing happiness constantly.

If I get a car, then I will be happy.

If I get this job, then I will be happy.

If I earn this much money, then I will be happy. Else, I won't be happy.

If there was never an "if," condition for your happiness, there will never be an "else" condition and you will always be happy naturally without any external factor or influence.[3]

The story is simple yet instructive. As we grow older and hopefully wiser, we understand happiness a little better. When we always presuppose an *if* condition to our thinking about happiness, then we are tied down to the acquisition of things. This is characteristic of Indian philosophical teaching on happiness: one must divest oneself from not only possessions but the desire for them as well.

A personal realization that love for others, my wife, my children, and other close friends was most important only came later as circumstances in my life changed. In the early years of my religious life (the ministry), I was told not to expect happiness as the world commonly understood the notion. Rather, I needed to enter into the suffering and death of Christ if I expected to be rewarded with a sense of contentment in the afterlife. Admittedly, I did not relate to the need to bring suffering into my life, and I moved on into what I thought was the best way to preserve my vocation but still be happy.

As a senior citizen, I have discovered that happiness can be considered a deep contentment and appreciation for life as it is experienced in the here and now. Perhaps we can call it a love of life. Love and life are common words with many levels of meanings, but certainly when we have experienced the two phenomena together, there surfaces a common understanding. We recognize it in older people who have had many experiences in their lives and accept the way they are in the present. They are at peace.

When inserting a religious conviction into the picture of happiness, things become somewhat more complex. In this book, I treat happiness from the point of view of a believing Christian. I realize that this approach does not address all the ramifications of what happiness could mean for every Christian, nor all the insights psychology may bring to the table. Admittedly, this could be an incomplete picture of all humankind's challenges with living a happy and fulfilling life. However, this chapter sets the scene for what occurs in the rest of the book. Happiness is a goal to which all people aspire in their lives. Here I treat such a state of mind from the stance of being spiritually and psychologically fulfilled. As I mature in age, I look to this form of contentment bringing me a special fulfillment in all aspects of my life.

What Is Spiritual Happiness?

Further to this idea is the question as to whether or not spiritual fulfillment brings the same amount of satisfaction and contentment as secular forms of satisfaction, such as the happiness experienced when there are children and grandchildren in a person's life. Timothy Wilson has some insights for us regarding happiness experienced from a religious point of view:

> Many studies show that religious people are happier than non-religious people. To get these benefits, though, you just can't go down to your local church, synagogue, or mosque and fill out a membership card. Religious people are happier only if they truly believe, and those beliefs are shared by their loved ones. If people have fragmented religious beliefs that are not well integrated into their overall lives, and if these beliefs are not supported by their loved ones, they are no happier than anyone else. Research also shows that people who believe in the devil and hell are less happy than people who do not. Apparently worrying that we might end up at Satan's side in everlasting flames confers less happiness than believing that—no worries!—we are guaranteed a spot in eternal Eden.[4]

Further to the point of being happy with what we believe, there could be some growing concerns about what we have learned through the influence of science. Doubts about our traditional beliefs may or may not bring us happiness in the future. Wilson has this to say:

> To a large extent, we acquire core narratives from our culture and parents and religions. We are provided

with a readymade belief system about the major questions in life, and for many of us, this is perfectly fine. Perhaps we went to church with our parents, have continued with that religion, and are happy with the spiritual guidance it provides. Other people, however, question their core narratives at some point in their lives, coming to believe that the religion they were brought up with does not provide all the answers, or that the prevailing cultural view about "the good life" is not for them. If they are lucky, they are able to find a new set of core beliefs that answer life's most basic questions.[5]

What is important in this discussion is that I am considering happiness from a spiritual point of view. Spiritual happiness means a movement toward self-fulfillment. If an individual moves ahead with a degree of happiness in today's world, it seems to me that such an individual is on a journey of some kind, searching for more satisfaction and happiness. I call that journey a quest. In some sense, then, we could say that in the context of spiritual happiness involving a quest, there is a tendency to look forward to a fulfillment, which is never complete. It is this idea I want to explore here. In one sense, we should never think of achieving complete satisfaction in any type of religious experience or experience of God. If any religious belief or institution says its proclamations result in complete satisfaction and happiness, I would say take another good look at that belief.

Happiness, as treated here, is more like an unending quest. In searching for God, we will have to live with an incompleteness, knowing that as our lives represent a journey, so also is our quest for ultimate fulfillment a journey in search of God. The early fathers of the church speak of happiness on earth for humankind as always an incomplete experience. We have St. Augustine saying, "Thou has made us for Thyself, O Lord, and our heart is restless until its rests in Thee."[6] The intent of St. Augustine was to show that only in heaven can a soul find its freedom from restlessness. However, freedom from restlessness does not offer a complete knowledge of God. Happiness for St. Augustine is not a surprise brought on by continually discovering God in new ways. However, this last statement is more in line with what I spend a good deal of time on in the following chapters of this book. We can and should find a sort of eternal happiness in the here and now.

Anthony Padovano speaks of a reality change in our view of God as we search for a continued understanding of fulfillment or happiness:

> God is not someone who grants our wishes; he is someone who fulfills our hopes. God does not make wishes come true; he makes reality work. He sustains us not in our whimsical desires but in our mature choices ... the difference between a man of faith and the man of no faith is the difference between a man who hopes for home and the man who wishes for a home.[7]

We can derive much from Padovano's words of wisdom on the relationship between what we wish for and what actually makes us happy in our spiritual lives. We probably will never be happy if we base our contentment on just getting what we wish for, as opposed to that which makes us truly happy in life. Although we may think that a desired package of wishes, if granted, will make us happy, the reality is that they will not bring the complete happiness that we desire. Our nature is such that we will simply continue to formulate more and more wishes needing to be granted.

Happiness does not result from the granting of a wish to be with God in heaven. It is the acceptance of the fact that a continual quest for God is the real happiness in our spiritual lives. The search or quest for God is the framework within which we need to work to be happy, not a package of wishes to be granted. The package of wishes we may have will constantly change. However, spiritual happiness is a continued love-search for God. Our idea of God is constantly changing as our faith in Him and our spiritual vision matures. Although we may feel deeply blessed with an experience of the presence of God, complete fulfillment and happiness will always appear to be ahead of us.

When we attach ourselves to certain religious proclamations, we need to know that there is not a doctrine, dogma, or spiritual edict that can ensure happiness in our lives. Following the dictates of a religious belief can only bring a temporary contentment, because our faith and knowledge of God need to mature as we grow in wisdom.

What I would like to say about spiritual happiness is that fulfillment in the continued search for God can and does result in some form of contentment. At this point, you are not expected to understand totally what I am saying and where I am going by what I have said in this chapter. I will say this: it is my conviction that somehow or another, real spiritual happiness constitutes a deep-seated love of life. It will take the rest of the chapters in this book to make sense to you why I have made this claim. At no time am I saying all happiness or any related sense of contentment and fulfilment in life must coincide with my understanding. Each person's search for God is always peculiarly unique. Love of life in the religious and mystical sense is as difficult to define and pinpoint as any common understanding that may or may not include a religious interpretation.

To summarize, many people believe that happiness is acquired and experienced when we are successful at some endeavor. If I have the right car, a winning lottery ticket, a great job, whatever it is, then I will be happy. But happiness does not come from being successful at doing or securing something. Rather, happiness is the forerunner to success. If we are happy, and when we are happy, then whatever goals we accomplish matter little or are of less consequence. In the course of this book, I will apply this insight in a different way. I will show how happiness, contentment, and satisfaction will, of their nature, never be completely fulfilled. This is good! I say this because our quest for God is never completed. Like a journey, our spiritual happiness will always carry a bit of unfulfilled satisfaction and contentment. Love of life in the present is crucial for experiencing happiness.

With each discovery we experience about the divine presence, a vast number of possibilities open up to us. These possibilities include not only increased personal happiness but a special kind of happiness we can share in community with others as well. In the final chapters of this book, I echo the Buddha's directive: "There is no path to happiness. Happiness is the path."[8] It is almost as if the journey in life is the destination. Living in the here and now is critical for arriving at happiness. Later, I apply this sense of happiness to what a new insight into eternity might mean.

inner peace

3

Is Our Initial Contact with God Satisfying? Probably Not.

I remember seeing an episode of *God Friended Me*, in which the main character's father, Arthur, had difficulty leaving his family home for another home with his future wife. Before his first wife's death from cancer, the family home meant everything to him. It was a place where he and his wife had raised their two children. Each room held memories; they were the places where the children slept, played, and grew to be successful adults. He just could not leave these treasured memories and move to another house with his new spouse.

The second wife felt she could not live in the original home because their relationship with each other would never mature. She told Arthur that they would never be able to move ahead with a new love relationship if his thoughts were always anchored to this one place. She made it very clear that they could never marry under such circumstances. Arthur could have kept the family home with the loving memories. However, walls, rooms, and doors did not themselves constitute the treasured memories. He finally realized that his love for his second wife would not mature and develop into something beautiful if he found himself focusing on past material things. As it turned out, he did decide in favor of his new wife and moved into another home. The new love experience was more important than the walls and doors that contained memories of the past. *The Now takes courage / Trust*

The Searching for God Conundrum

Arthur, the Episcopalian minister discussed above, is a figure who can show us how we need to move from one form of an attachment to a deeper and more meaningful one. In a similar way, we need to move from our adolescent ideas about God to an adult and more mature faith experience in His presence. My intent in this chapter is to show the need to move from ideas about God being *up there* and *out there* to spiritually real experiences of God being present in the here and now. In our early religious education, there was no need to distinguish between a physical and a spiritual presence. There was no need for showing an adolescent mind the difference between a spiritual God and a physical God (there is no physical God). As children, we are slow to understand anything except a physical location for God, and we think about heaven being up there and out there. Although we learned that God is spiritual, we still think of heaven as *somewhere* or *some place*. Children simply do not have the educational tools for sorting out the elements of this conundrum.

Have you ever found yourself looking around the corner for something, expecting that it should be in sight? When we find the object of our search, we experience a sense of relief and satisfaction. On the other hand, when we do not find the object of our search, a deep sense of frustration quickly arises in our minds, and we might get physically upset. We get the same feeling when waiting for a friend to pick us up and that friend does not arrive, either on time or not at all. When searching or waiting for something spiritual, like trying to find God in our lives, we encounter a similar kind of feeling. We might say, "Well, God is not there," or "I am not satisfied, but I will keep on looking."

Another way of looking at the conundrum is to admit that sometimes we do have a tendency to look for a sign that God is with us in the same way that we look for a person or something we can recognize. The problem is that we are in space-time, and our deity is not; He is outside of space-time, in a supposed eternity.

Consequently, as intense as our search is, it will never be successful. However, the search is what is important, because it represents a natural drive for fulfillment; only this is a spiritual search and not a physical one.

It is true that when first experiencing something as children, we rely totally on a sensory experience. Yet, as we approach adulthood, and in search of some spiritual entity or experience, sensory functions fall short or are incomplete and misleading, and oftentimes do not live up to our expectations. Some may think we can see God in His perfection through something that is in nature. However, our idea of God in creation is very much an image in our minds (not exactly physical), after we have received information from others through an instruction of some kind. For example, a beautiful landscape of autumn-colored trees, the northern lights in the darkness of night, a lake with the reflecting colors of the sky—all of these experiences are put together by the powers of our mind. We are the ones who create the image of something beautiful, just as we create the metaphor that mirrors the Godlike presence we enjoy in the wonders of creation.

What is fortunate now is that, with our ideas about the meaning of Godlike, we can make some headway in our search for a deity. Think for a moment of one of the most wonderful people you have met. Usually, your thoughts focus on the personality, the joyful and generous attitude, or other loving aspects of a Godlike person. It is not the facial looks, hair, stature, or other physical aspects that make this person Godlike. It is rather an immaterial aspect of their personality that reflects the image we have of a Godlike person stored in our mind.

Conceptualizing like this has helped me understand that the object of my search for God is not in the physical realm but rather the spiritual. When we search for a deity, it is true that the wonders of nature can oftentimes be instrumental in giving us a sense of wonder about God as we marvel at the gifts He has given us to enjoy. However, this perspective is limited. Such an experience usually begins and depends on the physical appreciation part. In nature, the autumn colors are there as a form of adaptation for survival. When we are searching for a God, we need to start with the internal image or idea we have in our mind. Instead of a spiritual journey to find God *out there*, to feel, see, hear, and smell in the physical world, the experience of His presence arises out of the power of our minds. The Holy Spirit will be revealed more and more as we journey in our quest for fulfilment.

Unless we see spiritually that the object of our search for God comes from within, then there is little doubt that we will always be searching for a God being an out-there entity. A spiritual search, as in searching for an experience of God, does not appear to have a finality to it. When experiencing God's presence, it is as if I am catching a passing glance, not able to grasp it in its entirety, similar to when I think of a Godlike person. Although a semblance of appreciation is felt, in that a new spiritual experience has been discovered, it does not offer an end to the search, and I must continually move on to something else, something more profoundly meaningful. If someone told me that he/she did have a spiritual experience, and it was of the very perfection of God, I would question it. Wouldn't you?

I would like to illustrate my point a bit further with another example: a love relationship. Experiencing God is like a love experience. When you are in love, deeply in love, the love experience is joyful and fulfilling. At the same time, it generates an ever-increasing appreciation for the object of that love as the years go by. Although there is a deep fulfillment, there is no finality in the experience of love. The same occurs in the search for God in our lives. We are bodily finite, but our search for God in our lives is not finite. The more we discover what God is like, the more fulfilled our lives could be. Although our images of God may be uniquely genuine, they are never complete; however deeply fulfilling our experience of God might be, it will always contain an element of a search.

Another way of looking at our challenge for a God search is to admit that humankind lives in an A to B world. We are confined to a space-time framework. We always expect to arrive at something or somewhere when engaged in a quest. There is a finality to our everyday objectives. We have a list of items to accomplish, and the objective is to achieve that finality. Generally, when we complete that list of items on the agenda, there is a sense of accomplishment. The problem with self-fulfillment is that it is not a space-time measurable challenge or condition. The quest or search for God is the same type of challenge. It is not an agenda that will offer a sense of completion. There is always a vast spiritual space opening up ahead of us, a vast dimension of the unknown to be discovered. All of these processes of a search begin with the earliest days of reasoning as a child. I will tell you a bit about my discovery of God.

Our Parental God

My initial experience of God is a good starting point. My discovery is likely more common and understandable to those who thought about spiritual things as they approached the age of reason. For me, all spiritual ideas came at a level that I could digest and understand at the time. I had no concept of what spirituality really meant. I will admit not much substance was there. My intention, at this point, is to show that we discover God as an entity formed in our minds by someone who is thinking for us. Bear with me as I explain what this might mean to you. In our early childhood, there are just too many sensual experiences flooding into our minds that make it impossible to generate something spiritual in nature. Any spiritual experiences always came from listening to stories that helped us form an idea about God being out there somewhere, in a place that no one really grasps.

There are many comical ways young people have viewed God and how they first thought about a deity in their lives. The following are just a few:

> "God is like a transformer. He can turn Himself into anything He wants."

> "When God gets mad, he lets out this thunder and throws lightening around."

> "God is either a woman or a man. I'm not sure."

> "God is a bearded guy with really big ears."

> "God's got an invisible head, and he floats in the garden. One side is night and the other side is day,

and God sees the owls and bunnies and butterflies. God also rides a motorcycle but he's playing hockey in Pasadena right now."⁹

One cannot help but chuckle at these examples. Nonetheless, as children, we accepted God as important and real, because our parents told us so. As a result, there is a parental image behind most children's idea of a God.

One of my initial personal encounters would be a good way to look at contacts with the supernatural. At three or four years of age, I can remember being interested in a picture on a wall of our home. It was a painting of a little child, maybe the same age as I, attempting to cross a raging creek by holding on to the railing of a swinging bridge. Above the child, there was a white-clothed guardian angel with beautiful, glistening wings. When I asked about the picture, my mother said we all have guardian angels to protect us in times of trouble, and that when worried about a danger ahead, we should pray to our own personal angel to protect us. I was told later on that there are some important people in the world who place themselves in extreme danger for any number of reasons; these people had archangels to guard them. I wanted an archangel some day!

Another image of God formed when I was looking at a picture book that my older brother or sister brought home from school. It was a drawing of a wide-faced man blowing wind and rain from a gathering storm cloud. This angry man was making it difficult for some fishermen in a small boat out on a lake. In my mind, God was a person of such serious power and strength that he controlled just about everything.

One time, when making a mess of our playroom, I heard my dad say, "You had better clean this up or, by God, you will wish you had." That did it. I now thought I knew who God was. I had to look for a protector when in danger and watch out when I was up to doing something foolish and wrong.

Before the first days at school, my discovery of God was of an amorphous humanlike person, somewhat distant but always present and ready to make judgments about good and evil actions. At the time, I had no idea that God was really the voice of my parents exacting final judgments on my actions. I did not know that notions of good and evil were commodities my parents took off their own memory shelves and fed to me like baby food for an infant.

My early-childhood prayer life was an extension of my idea of God being a parental God. As children, at home or at school, prayer was as common as sliced bread. We always said our prayers because it felt good to ask someone for something. Every once in a while, we got what we prayed for, and if we didn't, well, we assumed it was because we hadn't lived up to the expectation of our parental God.

There were times as a child when I truly felt that God was my guardian angel, very close and protecting me, similar to the force that protected the little child crossing the bridge in a storm. Gratitude for this protection expressed itself in an adolescent form of doing something nice for my parents or not taking candy away from my younger siblings. God was always as close as my parents were when I said my payers before bedtime. We always said prayers at night, because our parents expected it, and they usually asked if we had done our duty. Although I felt God to be close to me, I never felt He was within me; rather, He was an entity outside and up there somewhere, always looking down at me. It was definitely a parental God. Furthermore, I had no idea my initial experience of God was my parents' experience of God.

When kneeling in a pew, I had some experience of God's presence, based on what someone told me was up there, in the tabernacle or on the altar. God was always somewhere away from me yet present to me. There is nothing false about this assumption, because it came from a genuine childish act of faith. The problem is this: such an experience will not be sufficient in a modern Christian adult mind as a valid adult experience of God. What might be a satisfactory pedagogical stance for children will not satisfy a more maturing mind looking for the presence of God. What might be food for the infant will not satisfy the needs of an adult hunger.

Another insight into what we mean by God involves accepting the fact that we never actually see and understand something in exactly the same way as someone else. We could look at a landscape, mountain, or river view and never see it exactly the same way as our companions. The reason for this is obvious. Each viewer carries with him his own sensory abilities wired to his past experiences. He will be looking for one thing that pleases him, while I will be looking and finding something else in a landscape. It is well documented by psychologists that a witness in court is the least reliable evidence before a judge and jury. It is rare that what we describe in an incident is exactly how it happened. How much more so is our view of God and what God means to us as a unique and somewhat different entity.

The Judaic and Christian Vision of God

I invite you to look at what a vision of the Western concept of a deity over history might be. In the first place, we have the paternal God, not only the generator of all that is but the protector, the provider, and the guide as well. These characteristics are similar to what a father in a family would exhibit. Thus, in Hebrew history, lineages are preserved in myth form as paternally structured—that is, the principal leader of a tribe in charge of a given space in the Promised Land. The paternal God was solely masculine, dominant, and forceful. He was always in charge and responsible for events, fortunate and unfortunate, occurring in Israel. In fact, there are instances in which God *was* Israel.[10] The insight into this now is that the Hebrews were actually constructing their God. This would be a God who accommodates to the cultural practices of the time. For me, it was easy to accept the Hebrew concept of God as an adolescent, because this concept was paternal and understandable—that is, much like my parents but on a macrocosmic level. God was someone strong and all powerful yet still an entity out there in the big somewhere.

With the advent of Christianity, we have an addition to the paternal God, in that the figure of Jesus added a different and more personal perspective to the concept of God. This addition fulfills what can be described as a gentler approach. Jesus, the Son of God, represents the totality of what brotherly love should be. Jesus is the Son of God, and we are His brothers and sisters. Jesus's brotherly love is personal, not like the love and salvation of a nation or a male-dominated leadership, but rather like a deity that guides us closely, having taken on the aspects of humanity, walking in our shoes. The fraternal message of Jesus is one of love and acceptance, rather than war and domination; of lessons found in the Sermon on the Mount (the beatitudes), rather than a commandment to follow or perish.

Jesus was not a national figure but a self-taught teacher walking among the poor and downtrodden. The spirit emanating from Jesus was one of forgiveness, rather than punishment. The Jesus figure was one of understanding and love, rather than a promise to restore the kingdom of Israel to the Israelites. However attractive the Jesus mystique is to modern humankind, Jesus was still *out there* and as powerful as God Himself.

The late Middle Ages, even after the early fourteenth century, depicted the presence of a grandiose God, a deity exalted by an institution whose purpose was to show how a holy empire (Roman) was God's voice on earth. Such a kingdom necessitated a definite materiality, as well as the traditional expression of paternity and fraternity. Kingdoms arose, supposedly subservient to the holy kingdom of Rome, which was comprised of authority figures transmitting God's messages. Well after the appearance of monastic structures, the age culminated in the erection of magnificent Renaissance cathedrals and other similar tributes to an exalted being. With this understanding of God almighty, beyond anything we can imagine, God is still out there and powerful. With the industrial revolution, we have the beginning of a mechanistic God, perfect in that divine laws are perfect, and who had to reflect the determined and perfect laws of nature. All laws conformed to the divine laws revealed to us by God.

Traditional thinking about divine law changed with the introduction of quantum mechanics from the minds of great men such as Niels Bohr and Max Planck. With the original thinking of men like Albert Einstein, the educational prowess of the twentieth century dwarfed the successes of the creativity of the minds behind the industrial revolution. This resulted in the discovery that the accepted traditional laws of the universe simply could not explain the nature of both a macro and micro universe. The supposed deity was slipping quickly into irrelevance as an out-there God.

With the postcomputer age came the notion of a deity as being an amorphous force, such as that which empowered special characters in a *Star Trek* or *Stars Wars* movie. Hence, we have a quasi-deistic individual that needs the creativity and determination of special men, women, and outer space creatures to become real. This amorphous force at first glance could be considered having no institutional framework but is still somewhat religious in that its presence always indicated an altruism and peace for humankind, with the expression of both a physical and spiritual type of force. There are some other ideas about God that we need to address.

Have you ever thought about how we visualize God as a distant figure in heaven, apart from our minds? During childhood days, our parents would propose great ideas of a God up there, out and away from our limited sensory perceptions. We learned that He is in heaven with a select group of people who have been obedient and good at heart. Heaven was a place believed to be both material and immaterial at the same time, where we are meant to live in a glorified state with our bodies. By this, I mean God will take us somewhere to be with Him to enjoy eternity with a lot of good things (materiality). Furthermore, heaven is a place where there is no pain, suffering, or work to do. It is like heaven is a place where we can party forever and be happy to do so.

Some look at heaven as a place where we spend eternity looking at the splendor of God in all His goodness. I never ever really liked the idea of sitting around looking at a deity forever. There just had to be a place with something to do that I would like to do forever. Adolescent dreaming about God was encouraged by our parents and teachers. Such activity got us to thinking about God and eternal things. There just had to be a "pie in the sky when we die." In addition, we were instructed that God was not only out there and above us but also down here on earth, watching our every move and thought. Theologians have called this the doctrine of divine immanence and transcendence. It means that God is not only out there and away but also intimately connected to us here below. This doctrine has never been explained appropriately. In the next chapter, I will respond to this doctrine but with a new proposal.

The important idea that needs consideration near the beginning of this work is the way we think while being tied to a spatial framework. It is true we have no other framework in our ordinary lives, because we are confined to a space-time continuum. As mentioned earlier, it is difficult to visualize anything that is not drawn out in space that goes from A to B, and the length of time it takes to get from A to B.

When it comes to spiritual considerations, we allow ourselves to be locked into the same way of thinking. For instance, we automatically think of the incarnation (the coming of Christ) as an event that assumes a coming down from heaven into time, into some location we speak of in time. We laugh at ourselves and really want to say that Jesus did not come from somewhere in outer space, as if from another planet. We want to say something else but have difficulty saying just where heaven is, a heaven from which came the person of Jesus Christ. Our words use a special context, but we really lack the tools for telling someone about a deity, eternal and not bound within a space-time continuum. We simply cannot think about or speak about something eternal without describing it in a spatial framework.

In conclusion, what I have attempted to do in this chapter is to show how our initial understanding of God as a deity is formed from an outside source. We receive our ideas of God from instruction by our parents, supported by the insights offered in ancient biblical passages, and finally from the trappings of the Middle Ages into modern times. We are heirs to a variety of ideas about the nature of our creator, yet we still experience a nagging dissatisfaction. There just has to be more we can learn about God.

In the next chapter, I want to suggest a new paradigm about our relationship with our creator while, at the same time, using the same treasured words from our youth, but these will be words and thoughts with new and deeper meanings.

4

Can We Talk about Creation and Eternity in Our Search for God? Why Not?

We have discussed the possibility that most people believe heaven is a place in the same way that earth is a place. Heaven, for most, has to be somewhere and not just a construct of our minds. After we die, tradition says that we will be in heaven forever with our resurrected and glorified bodies. Theologians have struggled with this postmortem scenario and offer little comfort for the inquiring mind. Furthermore, no one we know has actually come back to talk about heaven. Our faith grounds our belief in the future life. It is our traditional belief that Christ rose from the dead, and from this belief, our faith is informed. Other than faith in an immortality of some kind, we have no idea what heaven is and our place in it.

There are two major topics discussed in this chapter, and these topics are alluded to in most chapters of this book. They are *creation* and *eternity*. We can refer to them as the beginning and the end of our mortal lives. Much controversy and talk surrounds what lies in store for us when we pass away. In our search for God, these topics will always come to mind. A friend once commented, in a humorous way, how people are obsessed with eternity, while at the same time are not too concerned with where they were before birth. Why are we so concerned about what happens after

death when we have no idea about a preconception experience? The point is well taken.

In this chapter, I am proposing that we look more closely at our existence in space-time, as opposed to where God is and our place in eternity. In ancient history, the ideas about God, creation, and eternity were discussed in various ways. In the book of Genesis, we have the writer stating that God created man in His own image. Hundreds of years later, we have Aristotle saying that men created gods after their own image. Sometime in between these two periods, the Greek poet Xenophanes said that if horses could create gods, their gods would be horses. Although Xenophanes was poking fun at the way certain religious believers think, he had a very good point as well.

Our way of knowing about God would be through a form of spiritual epistemology. Even so, this restricts us to a space-time framework for expressing our thoughts. What this means is we want to talk about God as being present to us now, not just how he was present to the apostles or talked about by early Greek philosophers. This requires an eternal point of view, and it is an impossible task. Since we presume there is no time in eternity, we cannot use our earthly measuring sticks for an immateriality that cannot be measured.

God is eternally present to all of creation. This means that at the same instant He is present to me, He is also present to the apostles. Another way of saying this is that God is the groundwork of existence for all Christians at the same instant that He is the groundwork of existence at the time of the apostles. In the context of eternity, for which there is no measuring stick, creation, incarnation, and redemption are simultaneous. However, in the context of time, such events had to be sequential. God events happened in time from our point of view, but I propose this is not so for God.

These thoughts can be a bit confusing, if not disturbing. Let me express myself using a visual form for clarification.

Old and New Paradigms

For purposes of moving this discussion along in a productive manner, we need to focus our search for God using a different paradigm or engage in what is called a paradigm shift.[11] A paradigm represents a specific set of concepts and thought patterns. A paradigm shift would mean a move away from one paradigm into another, and in this case, it involves another way of looking at the world and searching for God.

Oftentimes, a paradigm is called a worldview. The future of Christian belief, from our point of view, will always be an incomplete and unfulfilled paradigm or worldview because we do not know what the future holds for us. Being limited to space and time, there will never be an eternal component except in terms of a metaphor. The use of a paradigm in a spiritual context will always be somewhat inadequate. Being in time and space, we are never going to understand the eternal. I believe it is only by comparison that we can imagine what it might possibly mean to be eternal or like God. We can participate in faith, but our faith will never be complete, for we are and will never be eternal, as God is eternal. I believe that even in eternity, we will always be in search of the eternal—that is, in search of God. There will always be a quest for fulfillment of some sort.

The Traditional Paradigm

Discussing the need for a paradigm shift may be somewhat confusing. May I use an example of what I have in mind? Consider the graphic metaphor in figure 1 that represents a typical worldview of the meaning of the eternal. It is an analogy of the traditional expression of humanity's relationship to the eternal.

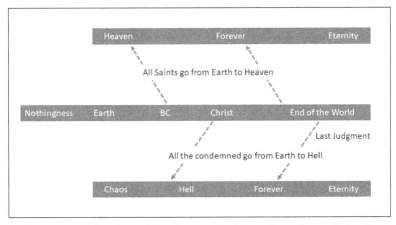

Figure 1. Traditional paradigm: the accepted view of creation and eternity

This graphic metaphor is a very close representation of the worldview of a Christian preacher from the time of Christ until now. The teaching church expressly proclaims that such a worldview is revealed to us through divine revelation (in the Bible and elsewhere) and cannot be challenged. Any challenge to this church teaching would be challenging the very authority of God.

I see several problems with this paradigm:

1. The configuration is a totally linear space-time framework. There is no place available for God's omnipresence and our evolutionary history.
2. The earth is created out of nothingness. This assumption goes against what we know from science.
3. The last judgment involves the end of the world and universe. Not only is the end of the world wrongly connected to an individual's actions, but matter in the universe could very well be eternal.
4. All sinners and saints go to their designated places. This idea is repugnant to the Gospel's sense of compassion.

The Spiritual Creation Wheel

I suggest we look at a different and more realistic graphic metaphor representing another worldview of our relationship (in space and time) with the eternal God. This next metaphor, shown in figure 2, is more in line with a scientific understanding of creation and a creator. This diagram, the spiritual creation wheel, is a visual representation of a new paradigm. It is still a construct of the mind and always an incomplete projection leading to more questions and possible interpretations. I will admit this is just another way we are trying to know more about the divine presence and what it means.

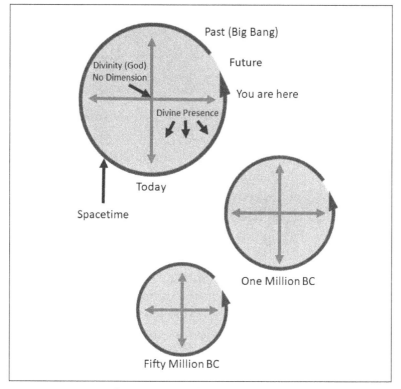

Figure 2. The spiritual creation wheel

Some initial points need to be made:

1. Similar to the first paradigm, it is a graphic metaphor, not the reality. It is just a way of explaining something about which we have little or no information.
2. We need to know that creation in science is not the traditional idea of creation out of nothingness. For science, our universe came to be from the big bang event, with minimal matter and incalculable amount of energy. Since most scientists maintain the universe did not arise out of nothingness, creation in this sense could be infinite.
3. Using the same words, I am structuring a different paradigm with novel implications for a believer who is still searching for God.

I invite you to look at the creation wheel while I now explain my metaphor in more detail.

The center of the circle is a point with no dimension, only location, and is equidistant from any point on the outer circle's circumference. The circumference of the outside circle represents the space-time continuum. Speaking by way of comparison, the inner point (God and eternity) is equally distant from any point on the outer circle, which represent our existence and the existing universe. For any point on the circle's circumference, we can say that it is restricted to its position at any time in its history. This is not so with divine presence. Although there is no future or past for God, there is only a single spatial contact for us with the inner point (God). We cannot live in the past and cannot at this time know much about the future. We can only surmise, with an intelligent guess, about the inner point's effect on humankind's past or past events (events described in history books, Bible, etc.). We have no idea about the inner point's contact with us in the future.

Now consider the shaded space around the arrows inside the large circle as revealing the power of God, His presence and influence. God's presence is constant, unending, eternal, and everywhere. The inner space is the same from the point of view at the center, but from any point on the outer circle (in space and time), there is no way of knowing this. Using this space-time creation wheel metaphor requires that the wheel gets larger as time goes on, because space-time requires distance. To incorporate continual divine presence with space-time in the form of a graphic metaphor requires a circular drawing. Hence, God's presence can be considered the same at all times in history and the same at all points on the circle. God is in everything, and everything is under His creative influence.

Boethius, a late-fifth-century Christian philosopher, entertained some of the same thoughts as I have proposed in the creation wheel. He taught that God, being eternal, is not in our time but is necessarily present to the past, present, and future. For Him, humankind knows the past only as past events, the future as assumptions of what might be ahead, and is only aware of what is happening now. Unfortunately for us, Boethius was more concerned with the proper translation of Plato and Aristotle, along with defending the concept of free will, than some of the implications inherent in his ideas about God being eternal. Also, the big bang and modern science's understanding of creation were not part of his life and vocabulary.[12]

The Christian church has always preached about God's immanence (forever close) and transcendence (forever apart) but has not really explained the ramifications of such teachings. Christian tradition can only speak in its own time of an event believed to have happened in the past or expected to be happening in the future. If we say God is eternal, then, since we are not eternal and really do not know anything for sure, we could accept the creation wheel as something worth thinking about.

Given that my second graphic metaphor is credible, we can draw the conclusion that there is possibly no such thing as God's intervention into time and space, because God is always present to all points on the outer circle at the same time. Why would divine intervention be necessary? For some, to deny divine intervention will be difficult, but we can address this concern with the idea that God is always present and exposed at any given time to any point of humankind's existence. If we draw this idea out to its logical conclusion, we would need to question the occurrence of miracles and other spiritual phenomena as being anything other than physical events that are explainable phenomena, given enough scientific and technological scrutiny into each case.

You might ask why I am discussing at length the topic of creation and eternity. Allow me to explain my conclusions more clearly by looking at the implications of the creation wheel:

1. The deity is present to every instance and place in our space-time continuum and is the very ground of our total being (existence).
2. When discussing divine intervention on behalf of someone using the spiritual creation wheel, it would be as if the deity were intervening upon itself. Since God is eternally present to all of creation, it seems irrational to alter, change, or bring something else into a time-picture already grounded in His own eternal presence. It would be like a deity changing its own eternal presence at any given place in the history of the universe. On our part, we can always ask God to make changes on behalf of a created being or on behalf of a group. But how can we ask

the eternal being to change its own ground of being in the universe? To clarify this point, we could say, "God does not make junk, and God is forever present to everything."
3. There is no room for an eternity in hell or an eternity in a heaven (I treat this subject more fully in a later chapter). To look at heaven as a place where God rewards a good life is no more realistic than a hell where a god punishes an evil person forever. In other words, I am dispelling a heaven or hell in the traditional sense. We need to discover the kingdom of God in the here and now, in our hearts and in the hearts of a believing community. In later chapters, I will explain how I believe we can achieve the qualities of the eternal in our lives right now.
4. It is up to the individual believer to imagine what happens after death. Heaven and hell (places where) are not the important and predominant goals we should be aiming for in this life.

The kind of paradigm I have proposed will most certainly represent a real shift in the way we think. When thinking about treasured and ancient beliefs in the matter of God, we often fail to examine not only what the object of our search must be like but also what concessions need to be made regarding traditional ideas such as miracles. What we have actually thought to be intervening instances of God's acts on our lives from creation to eternity are probably just unexplained phenomena in our search for God. This may be a hard pill to swallow. The search for God in our lives must go on; we must always be open to new discoveries as we attempt to find a resolution to dilemmas like creation and eternity.

Looking at the two paradigms together, we can still maintain certain treasured beliefs. In our prayers, we should still accept the presence of God in our lives. However, we can replace our constant petitioning with a mindfulness that lets the Holy Spirit be our strength, rather than asking God to dismiss upcoming obstacles. This strength allows us to meet any challenges coming forward in our lives. Our strength is the Holy Spirit. The Holy Spirit works within us, not outside of us.

Besides being eternal (as both paradigms show), we acknowledge God as all knowing, all-powerful, and all benevolent. Why does Christian tradition say this about God? Tradition says this because these are ideal qualities that we cannot possibly possess. Therefore, we believe only a deity can possess them and must possess them. Our lives will continually be involved with discoveries and quests like these that lead us closer to understanding the characteristics of our God.

Beginnings and Endings

At this time, it would be appropriate to reiterate one last thought about creation and eternity. With regard to creation, the traditional meaning is to bring about something from nothing. This is not science's view of creation. Although the term *creation* is used in science, the understanding is much more sophisticated. Given the interconvertibility of mass and energy as expressed in quantum mechanics, it is conceivable that matter did not exist at the beginning of time (time is used loosely here). But energy and probably dark matter always did exist. Some scientists espouse the theory that matter is really the outward and visible expression of energy.

With the big bang, the birth of matter from energy is not a scenario similar to the creation narrative in the Bible. Energy is a physical reality in our universe, and though we cannot prove its eternal nature, many discoveries in quantum mechanics indicate that, in its dark form or light form, energy has always been around. Although our universe exists at this time, it may very well not be the only one. Our universe may be just one of many that have occurred or will occur over time.

I can now ask many questions about eternity and how an eternal figure can fit into my search. In my quest, what more can I learn about my God? Looking at the creation wheel discussed earlier, although the outer rim of the wheel is in touch with God's presence, we do not thereby influence God. As long as we exist in a space-time continuum, we will not fall into the eternal or eternity. This leaves much food for thought. As in the traditional paradigm, the creation wheel is only another way of looking at topics such as creation, eternity, immortality, and God's presence in our lives. Our faith is what offers us a way of bridging the gap between time and eternity.

As we move along in evolutionary history, we will become more knowledgeable about God. However, we have been taught that it is only our immaterial qualities that can possibly persist forever. What are those immaterial qualities? Given the gradual move away from a traditional idea of a soul created out of nothing, we must continue to investigate the miraculous activity of the mind. The idea of the soul being immaterial, created, and immortal is an analogy only and not the reality. We will continue to search for the meaning of God in our lives through the quasi-infinite capacity of the mind within the brain and the mind's power to learn more and more.

In conclusion, this discussion has no doubt either introduced a deep sense of confusion within you or a sense of enlightenment about how to define, discover, and continue our search for the divine presence in our lives. I hope the following chapters will help to clarify for you why my search for God needed a new paradigm to respond to what I have experienced.

This chapter could be a challenging one for many. However, I want to say my life has been enriched with science and the introduction of a new paradigm into my prayer life and daily activities. I feel deeply the presence of God in everything I achieve or fail to achieve. These new insights require me to be very careful with what God has given me and how, in my later years, I need to be more sensitive to my own well-being and that of others. This way of looking at my spiritual life has taken me away from a focus on the hereafter in terms of a place where, to the kingdom within my own being. I have now begun to put new meaning into traditional words and have used creation and eternity as only two examples of what discovery and a continual search can bring about in my life. In a sense, there is no end to my life. I believe we need to quit thinking about what lies ahead after this life and focus on the here and now. We should keep our quest going. Our search should never end but begin once again with discovering new insights as we become more and more fulfilled with the divine presence, the Holy Spirit.

5

Are Divine Revelation and Inspiration God-Given Truths? Yes and No.

For two millennia, the Christian church has been very adamant that its teachings about God have their origin in some kind of divine authority. The church teaches that humankind could not have conceived of the nature, workings, and expectations of a deity without some sort of revelation in the course of Judeo-Christian history. The possibility that humankind can be intelligent enough to discover God under its own power has always been out of the question. Divine revelation and inspiration must always be in the mix when discussing religious belief.[13] But I believe it is time to look at divine revelation and inspiration in a new way. In this chapter, I wish to propose a more meaningful approach, which is in line with what we know about human intelligence and its capability. We can in some ways, and under our own power, discover what the presence of God means in today's world.

The *yes* in the title of this chapter has to do with how the divine presence participates in our new spiritual insights. The *no* has to do with the supposed unchanging truth of what has been revealed. We can still understand and treasure our spiritual gifts of *what* was revealed (revelation) and *how* these gifts of faith were revealed (inspiration). The challenge is to figure out how these gifts enhance our faith today.

There are several arguments in the church's defense of the idea that it alone has the divine authority to interpret what revelation means and how inspiration takes place in the minds of sacred writers and preachers. The most common defense originates from the belief that man has fallen and could do nothing good without the saving grace of God. The church enters in as the provider of this revelation that humanity has fallen and needs the saving grace of God. Therefore, the church has the divine authority from God to legislate and enforce any proclamations on how we can now be saved by God. Not only are we fallen in nature, but we are constantly violating the natural order of things set in place by God Himself.

The second defense is that the universe exhibits an absolute order in the cosmos that we must follow, and this is called the natural order of things from which natural law is derived. Natural law has, at its core, a universalistic philosophy. This means there are laws existing outside our minds, which are universal in nature. The existence of universals (principles of existence) are there to guide us and exist independent of our own fragile being. Whether universals exist is highly debatable. The supposed natural law is the strongest defense for traditional thinkers because it is obligatory in nature and binds all human beings within a moral framework, spelled out carefully by the Christian church. If not absolutely adhered to, disorder, chaos, and damnation are believed to be the outcome. The church claims itself as the teaching authority of God in all matters relating to faith, reason, and morality.

If we look closer, the problem with the church's thinking on the matter is that there is no preordained, preexisting law out there in the universe that carries with it an obligatory connotation.

Instead, what we perceive are patterns and consistencies in nature that are noticed, discovered, and stored in the mind. From these patterns, we form concepts. It is out of these concepts that laws of the universe are formulated. In today's understanding, these formulations are called laws of nature, not natural law. Laws of nature are much like formulas existing in the mind, written down on paper, or stored on a computer. These laws are verifiable formulas built on the discoveries of patterns, from which predictions are made. This is how science functions today. Laws are derived from the mind researching the patterns and consistencies found in nature. These laws of nature may change as science finds better and more sophisticated measuring sticks.

Natural law has been a construction of early theologians for use in directing the actions of Christian believers. These laws have their germinal forms in ancient Greek philosophy, which had notable gods and demigods controlling the lives of human beings. If gods were up there somewhere in the heavens (for example, the Roman god Jupiter), then there had to be regulations that humankind must understand and follow in order to appease and make supplications to these gods.

The current teachings about the nature of God and the different forms He takes are derived from ideas worked out by the early theologians for the benefit of the devout believer. The point of their teaching about the nature of God is to get humankind back on the track to salvation. But there is not a single idea we have about God that does not take the same course or process in our brain that all fabricated ideas, formulas, and laws take when leading us to an insight about anything.

What we know about God has its origin in the mind of the believer in the distant past. Ancient thinking says that if humans cannot do something that needs to be done, then there must be a God that will, upon supplication, accomplish or fulfill that need. It is important to realize that our fabrications or concepts about God are not paltry or unimportant. They are important because whatever they are, they are part of the basic definition process that leads to further discoveries and quests for fulfillment. We are slowly achieving our goal of being enveloped in the majesty of the divine presence we call God by discovering important insights from past revelations.

In community worship, we share the presence of God within us. Our prayers and songs illustrate the ways in which we understand the presence of God in our lives. God's presence is the power behind our drive to learn more about Him. We discover God's presence in our own life experiences. Although what we know may come from our minds, these experiences are not totally of our own creation. We are sharing these experiences with others in common worship. Common worship is crucial for further discovery of God as He reveals Himself to us and, at the same time, inspires us to even more fulfilling insights.

Consequences for Revelation and Inspiration

If what I have proposed is closer to making God's presence to us more credible in our world today, what value is there in the traditional understanding of revelation and inspiration? I can say that there is always an important value to what our forefathers have handed down to us. In the context of early Christian times, God's presence was revealed in ways that believers could understand and accept. Revelation took place because the people of God were truly inspired. The whole religious process of believing within a community took place, and it endured for centuries. The difficulty I have with this process is that its source is based on an unquestionable truth. The truth would be absolute and originate from the authority of God's word. This means God handed down statements that cannot be challenged. This line of thought would be a source of contention for me.

A crucial part of preserving revelations and inspirations is that the process has to be going on even to this day. However, at this time, we cannot challenge doctrines and dogmas because they are sourced in the deposit of faith (given to us as revealed), and that ceased with the death of the apostles and early fathers of the church.

However, I believe revelation is what we have discovered about God at any given time in our lives in the here and now. Furthermore, inspiration is, in my mind, a force (the Holy Spirit) arising from an evolutionary process in discovering God. Within us, there is much more revealing going on about God's presence in today's world than what was revealed in the first century CE. We need to continue this legacy of God's revealing presence today in our own lives, not just the legacy we received from the ancient Hebrew prophets and early disciples of Christ.

In the centuries after the early disciples sat at the foot of Jesus, changes and adaptations occurred all the time. The church has constantly been putting new meanings to old words and concepts, dogmas, and doctrines. What I am doing is putting the process where it belongs, not necessarily in the institutional church but also within the power of our minds. It is not my intent to discard the ideas of revelation and inspiration but to redefine them, rediscover them, and continue the journey to find out more about our beliefs arrived at from these two sources. However, the content of these two sources should never be set in concrete—fixed and never changing—but should undergo a constant rediscovery and revision in light of the context of our time. Christianity needs to constantly move ahead and mature in knowledge and appreciation of what the presence of God means for us today.

Revelation and inspiration in this new understanding need not require a divine intervention of some sort. Revelation and inspiration leading to truth are discovered out of the power of the mind. This does not mean God's presence and powers are excluded but that out of the inquiring mind come the revelations and the inspirations that we treasure. Revelations about God are discovered. Inspirations arise out the Holy Spirit working within us in the here and now.

It is my intent here to show the need to revisit traditional teachings and offer a chance to look at them in a new light. At no time do I suggest discarding anything that should be treasured. My purpose is to put a new meaning to how God reveals and inspires the faithful today. If we are to continue our search for God, we must refuse to accept edicts under the guise of an unchallengeable authority. To accept on faith every dogma, doctrine, or edict about God does not work with me as a scientist. Please bear with me as I move this discussion along, leading to more insights on revelation and inspiration.

What Are the Revelations behind Inspired Biblical Stories?

There is something fairly simple, oftentimes overlooked, and yet important in understanding our faith. Biblical stories of the past carry a true value. However, this value can be lost in telling the story. The true value I speak of is the meaning behind the story. The stories found in the Bible have always been modified somewhat over the centuries, but the reason for telling the story could very well remain the same. A story is told to help us understand we need God in our lives. The divine presence grounds our reason for being right now, and we need to accept and enhance this presence with new as well as old stories.

As small children and adolescents, we were told Bible stories about God and His relationship with humankind. Whether it was the Adam and Eve episode, Noah and his ark, or other notable figures in the Old Testament, most of these stories were interesting to learn about. However, we were told the stories were the absolute truth as revealed in all its aspects. This may work when we are children, since there is a great deal of learning and enrichment available from these stories. As we mature, there must be a deeper understanding of what is meant by the truth in the story as revealed to us. There is a perennial value to each story, and less important is the historical context. What I mean by this is that the understanding of an episode by a six-year-old should not be the extent of the understanding of a thirty-year-old. For example, as adults, the veracity of the Adam and Eve episode must be explored differently, because our faith needs to continually move forward as we mature. Adam and Eve represent us, who are not only capable of sinning but actually do sin, and we need the Holy Spirit to empower us to do good things. This lesson to be learned must never stand still. It needs to move forward and be understood within the context of our time.

As our faith tells us, the Bible says something to both young and old. Yet our faith must be provided with something more enriching. If our faith does not move forward as we mature, then we will, sooner or later, suffer what is called a form of cognitive dissonance—that is, a tension in our lives brought about by upholding something in our hearts that is contradictory to what our minds know is not the absolute truth. There is always truth of some sort we learn from a Bible story, but a moral lesson may be the extent of it in some instances.

Just as our concept of God evolves as we mature, so also must our understanding and acceptance of passages in the Bible change. If this understanding does not develop, we will fall into the same abyss that fundamentalists have found themselves. They maintain every episode in the book of Genesis or elsewhere in the Bible is the absolute literal truth of the matter, because the Bible came from the unquestionable authority of God. What results is a life spent trying to prove things to be the absolute truth in every sense, rather than to glean the truly important life-enriching aspects of a story in the Bible. Unfortunately, it is too often the case that the tools we use to sharpen our faith as adults are sadly lacking that important function.

When discussing the valuable aspects and concepts we have about God, we must always be clear about the religious values set before us. The concepts we have about God are transient and ephemeral. These ideas and experiences may be very fluid or long-lasting, and they can help us through many challenges we have with our lives and faith. However, if we are continually searching for God, our ideas and concepts about an eternal being will need to change within the context of our lives. The concepts about God have changed for me. In my quest for fulfillment, I can treasure my past ideas and experiences but never ever be personally satisfied with them. That is the way it should be, since I am always on a journey, and the landscapes and paths that I travel will always be changing. It is out of the journey that the quest for God becomes more and more meaningful but never ending.

I have tried to answer the question of the yes and no portion in the title of this chapter. The experience of God in our lives is a terrific force for good. This force is not altogether our own making. It arises as an expression of a divine presence (inspiration). Our perceptions about God (revelations) are not only handed down to us over the ages, but new perceptions should continually arise out of our discovering minds as well.

In the next chapter, I will continue my search for God through the maze of traditional religious myths and revelations.

6

Are Myths and Mysterious Revelations True? Not as We Have Traditionally Believed.

You have probably heard stories of highly mysterious and almost incredible events in the past. In Roman literature, we have Romulus and Remus feeding at the breasts of a she-wolf for survival. Greek myths abound with human heroes, such as Hercules, who performed incredible tasks for his king and was raised to the level of a god. Most ancient religions tell innumerable myths to explain why worship of certain gods is necessary, or as explanations of why humankind suffers through so many calamities and wars.

The Bible is filled with tales of important people who performed feats of bravery and fidelity in the presence of God. From my childhood, I learned all kinds of such stories, taken from scripture and elsewhere. My impression at the time was that these stories were about real events, but I have now learned they were only stories that were intended to convey some kind of lesson to be learned. In this chapter, my intent is to show how important it is to move from a focus on the reality of biblical myths and revelations to the reason for telling the story. In learning more about God,

I believe we need to turn from the story and look at the reasons why the story is important. You may question whether the story is true, but you must also ask if a biblical story can provide more knowledge about God.

In ancient times, when most people were illiterate, stories were passed on orally as a teaching tool for later generations to treasure. Past biblical stories were part of a faith experience, a good way to learn more about God, though the details of these stories were oftentimes altered. The God of the ancients was an exacting God with a vengeful nature. If the chosen people were to survive, obedience to His rule of law had to be absolute, and disobedience led to enslavement and death by the conquering infidels. In most instances in the Bible, there was always some lesson behind the story of a great feat or huge failure. Through the telling of myths, the believer learned some important beliefs about God. We can learn more about God even when we fabricate myths, because the myth can generate more questions and discoveries. I believe we can learn more about living in peace as we discover a myth to be a revelation of a moral truth or lesson on how to love one another.

Most theologians understand myths as stories with a moral attached to them. There is always some kind of truth in a myth; it is an educational tool used to teach and instruct us how to act properly. We learn the lesson that came from some kind of failure involving a character or two in the mythic story, and, if elevated by teachers of the faith to the level of an historical event, these stories can generate questions as to whether that event actually happened.

Unfortunately, in religious tradition, myth is often put on the level of an actual event. Consequently, theologians in the past delved into the intricate depths of what this must mean, and teachers attempted to explain how these events could have happened. For example, a rainbow appearing after a heavy rainfall traditionally reminds us of the flood at the time of Noah and is considered to be a sign that God promised such a flood would never happen again. Instructors went to great effort to explain what the story meant and, because it was true, why it must be important. Later on, volumes of religious works were written to explain what the story could mean to a believer. We call this the realm of mysticism and mystery. Truths about God were discovered and explained from shared biblical stories. What the early Christians learned from these stories also generated many theological questions. However, looking at the innumerable stories, most of them tell us simply that we are capable of sinning, we actually do sin, and we need God to fix things right.

How Is Original Sin a Myth?

[handwritten annotations: "never existed", "Original Blessing"]

In the letters of St. Paul, we have the beginnings of a very interesting belief that relates to an ancient biblical story about the coming of the promised Messiah (our Savior). What could have been a powerful metaphor for Christian instruction quickly became a firm belief leading to the creation of a doctrine promulgated by the church even to this day. This is the doctrine of original sin. Adam and Eve, as the first parents of humankind, are pictured as figures who disobeyed God's commands. Jesus arrives on the scene as being the second Adam, setting our relationship with God once again on a firm footing. Because of the first sin of Adam, all of humanity now shares in this fallen nature of the first parents. The only way to be in favor with God is through the saving actions of Jesus Christ, our Messiah. The story of our first parents is thought to be necessary and true in every sense of the word. What other reason could there be for needing a Savior in the person of Jesus Christ unless we have fallen from grace?

In Adam, humankind sinned for the first time and is guilty of the first or original sin. The story of our first parents has its origin in an ancient Mesopotamian myth predating the time of the Babylonian captivity of the Israelites. This story became a strong instrumental tool for rabbis to teach about our fallen nature and need for God. What was supposed to be the foretelling by the prophets of a promised Messiah who would come and save the nation Israel from its enemies, now in Christian tradition became a longing for a Messiah who would save us from our sinfulness. Unfortunately, a literal understanding of the story of Adam and Eve became the focal point, in place of a truth about God's relationship to humankind.

Original sin is not mentioned in any of the creation narratives in the book of Genesis. However, in Christian tradition, because of the first sin, we were taught that we are fallen in nature and need a Messiah (redeemer). We need to be saved. The point or moral behind the myth, as I see it, is that we need God, not that we have fallen from grace. In our search for God, we find out that we really do need Him. God is the one who puts sense and purpose into our lives. As agnostic as we might be toward religion, we must admit an urge to believe in something beyond our grasp.

The problem with the Christian traditional understanding of the Adam and Eve narrative is that the fall of humankind becomes the focal point. Few theologians pay attention to the fact that in ancient Hebrew writings, there are at least five instances of humankind's fall from grace.[14] By the fourth century CE, it was the mystery of the first sin, original sin, that becomes the important theological thought. So entrenched is this mystery that most Christians, when approached with the facts regarding the evolution of Homo sapiens, suffer a cognitive dissonance between the facts of human evolution and the importance of original sin. The implication from realizing the mythical nature of the Adam and Eve story leads to a question such as, "Then why did Christ have to die on the cross, and why do we need to be redeemed?"

The Christian theological emphasis has been focused on the mystical and mysterious idea of the first sin, and consequently, the doctrine of original sin now relies on the supposed reality of a myth, even though the story is only a fabrication originating from many religious traditions. Ancient traditions attempted to resolve the question as to why there are evil and horrible things happening in the world. In Christian tradition, the answer is that humankind is fallen, and we do sin against our neighbor.

The problem with modern theological thought is that stories, since they are believed to be literally true, always need to be explained in some fashion. Consequently, myths in the Bible oftentimes have become the supposed reality, true in every sense of the word.

Myths still carry a dominant aura of mystery and, although mysterious, are part of the believing experience in our lives. For some of us, they are enough to help us see why we need God in our lives. That is fine! But if we believe, based on someone else's authority, that the doctrine of original sin is based on a real event, we will certainly stumble in our search for a deeper understanding of the presence of God in our lives. The evolutionary principles documenting humanity's origin from ancient primates has to be a necessary component of our search for God. We are not fallen angels but risen primates.[15] We actually learned how to survive by discovering that immoral actions need to be replaced by fairness in order to live in peace and safety with our neighbor.

Understanding God Is Not How We Experience God

We have just looked at biblical stories in terms of the value each one has for educating the believer about God's relationship with humankind. Although these stories are, for the most part, creations of religious leaders, they offer true value for sustaining young minds with ideas that can lead to further discoveries about God our creator.

I think it is important now to understand that what we have learned about God from biblical tradition is not the same as our experience of God. When we were little children, our parents and teachers were the sole providers of information leading us to form our idea or concept of God. As a child, I cannot remember having any initial experience of God or His presence. I was only concerned with the tactile, filling myself with what I could touch, eat, and so on. I definitely remember anthropomorphic images of a supposed supreme being, such as a majestic face blowing clouds and storms upon the earth, or an angel-like figure guiding small children through a dangerous walkway or trail. All of these images in my mind eventually (I cannot say exactly when) became sources for the birth of an experience of God.

Early in my life, it was difficult to think of God as anything or anyone different from the ideas I had received in my childhood. When I reached the age of reason, around the age of seven, I began understanding God as an experience. I know this to be the case because I would start talking to Him, praying not in a rote manner but through a conversational acceptance of Him. By this, I mean that God was someone whom I could talk to, ask for things, or even complain. Although there was no way I could have formulated the object of my prayers as a discovery of God, nonetheless, it was an experience that went beyond the simple ideas, images, and pictures presented to me earlier in my childhood. Looking back on my initial experience of God, I can now formulate my discovery of God as a special presence that was just there. It was all that I could say about the experience at the time.

The point I am making is that my experience of God was not reducible to the concepts given to me by my primary educators. These experiences of God indicated that I had actually discovered God in my life. My discovery of God was not restricted to images, concepts, or anything on the level of an intellectual nature but a discovery of a special kind of person residing in my heart. Of course, it was not until much later in life that I was able to distinguish what I was taught as being radically different from what I experienced.

As I approached adulthood, I was actually discovering God on my own, and God's likeness became more than just a fabrication of my mind. For me, this was a very genuine experience. When moving into teenage life, all the experiences associated with those years of confusion and uncertainty about myself, life, people, and the concepts I received from parents and educators about God did not live up to what I needed to know about God as a personal experience. The traditional idea of God as one being up there, and the associated doctrinal ideas, did not and could not fit into to my experience of God. What was offered in classes was knowledge, not experience.

I am sure that a good number of my peers in high school felt the same way, and we were patiently waiting to be out from under the watch and care of parents. Attending church and listening to preachers was troublesome and boring. Many of us had a notion of God but not an experience that fit well within the framework of traditional parental concepts. My maturing experiences of God, or whatever they were, began to fall or leave behind, piece by piece, my childhood ideas of a previously defined God.

As our faith experience grows, it is important that new concepts and ideas of a deity enter into the picture of a God who is credible—that is, believable for us at our stage of life. As we mature and put a certain value to previous concepts, we begin to put aside those concepts that do not fit with our growing experience of God. It is not beneficial to discard traditional ideas as if they have no value. Some early beliefs are just not as important to us in our lives now. Remember, the experience of God is not the same as our ideas about Him. This becomes clear when we revisit some humorous quotes from expressions related to what we were told by our parents. These are definitely hand-me-downs and, as previously discussed, are purely conceptual for the child.

> God has a ring around His head, and he created Himself.
> God lives up in heaven, and heaven has houses and stuff.
> God lives inside us, so my doctor has seen God when he cuts people open.
> God wears one side of himself in pink with a skirt, and the other side is blue with pants.
> God sits at a big desk in the clouds and watches us everywhere.
> My mom talks to God when we need more money.[16]

As I was experiencing adolescence, my idea of God developed on a much more sophisticated level. I began to experience a deity not reducible to childhood concepts and teachings taught to me in my earlier years. My understanding of God as a teenager began to focus more and more on my experience of God rather than on a

God with physical characteristics. It can be very understandable that our initial ideas about God cannot live up to the demands of our experience of God as we grow into a more mature and rational life of adulthood. As we mature through our concepts of a God into an experience of God, the effect is similar to the difference between night and day. To me, concepts about God (doctrines, dogmas, etc.) could never live up to the experience of the presence of God in my life.

Rather than putting human shapes and figures to God, a mature belief must let a divine presence take hold, a presence arising not from the conceptual but from a discovery experience generated from our entire personhood. While a childhood understanding of God is a transfer of ideas given by someone else, an adult experience of God is more like an awareness of a presence coming from within oneself, one's whole being.

What makes this awareness of God an important experience for me is that it is a unique experience tailored to my own personality. Religions that have not undergone an institutionalized process demonstrate an initial idea of divine presence sooner than most organized religions. A good example would be indigenous groups that have a quasi-pantheistic orientation. By this, I mean a spirit hovering over all of nature: the wind, the snow, the eyes of animals, trees, and so on.

Discovering the Qualities of God

There is a common thread of understanding, although hidden for the most part in our early lives, that begins to solidify into three important insights as we move into more mature experiences. This would be that God is all-powerful, all knowing, and all benevolent (good). Even as children and adolescents, many of the descriptions of God given to us pointed to these three common characteristics of a deity. These descriptions can become real and true experiences, indicating that we have begun to discover God not as an entity out there but as an experience arising from within ourselves. What is important is that, as one matures, there is a gradual movement away from understanding God being real only because of a given story in the Bible. It is the lesson or moral behind the story, fable, or myth that is valuable for us.

For most adults, the challenge is to recognize the hidden truth behind a biblical story and to see it as an instrument for teaching and learning specific morals, leading to appropriate action. However, at times, we must admit to a desire for the intricacies of a story to be true. It seems to bring more comfort because there is the semblance of a resolution offered. It is comforting to recall the many times we listened to these biblical stories as children.

At this point, we can apply the value of discovering the qualities of God mentioned above. A person has, so to speak, traveled all around the world and come back to the original place (in this instance a story) and sees that place for the first time. What is important in the discovery portion is something different from the story (myth). Being all-powerful, all knowing, and all benevolent tells me much more about God than does the story of creation, Noah's ark, or the Tower of Babel.

The qualities of God are much more generic and more applicable to our own personal experiences than any story in the Bible. This is good, but now the believer has discovered that conditions such as evil, death, and natural disasters will lead us to newer insights into the qualities of God. This process leads us to ask serious questions. How can a deity who has all these good qualities allow such horrible things to happen in the world? What a discovery of

God does is lead us to the realization that we cannot put blame on God for all the unfortunate things that happen in the world. So we are invited by a discovery (a personal experience of some kind) to move into a quest to find answers to a question or dilemma. In this sense, not being satisfied (fulfilled) by what a discovery means, we plod ahead for further insights and discoveries about God. In our mind, there has to be a resolution to the conundrum of God being all good and the many bad things that happen in the world. So the search goes on.

As I conclude this chapter, some important reminders surface. I initially focused on the nature of myth and some formal revelations passed on as tools for education in religious groups. I showed examples helpful in understanding myths, not as depicting real events but more as stories containing lessons to be learned. I then attempted to show that how I first understand God in concept is not how I experience God in a maturing faith act. Having understood that myths convey more of a moral point than historical reality, I discovered what I was taught about God is not the same as my experience of God. There is more to God than what a myth or revelation offers my faith. Finally, thoughts about God revealing Himself in myths and revelations lead to discovery of certain qualities that do not contradict what I have learned about Him in the past but nonetheless offer a new perspective.

I admit there is an ongoing challenge in my mind that what I believe to be a divine presence in my life could not be a kind of presence that allows so many tragic events to happen in the world. What I have experienced about God does not align with all the events that turn this world upside down. Consequently, what I experience is not all there is to an explanation of God, and I need to persevere in my search for God in new ways. Slowly in our lives, we are learning what faith as a gift (virtue or power) truly means for us as adults.

In the next chapter, I hope to explain how defining, discovering, and searching are necessary to solve questions about God, His divinity, and the divinity of His Son. Although controversial, my ideas flow from what I have shared with you about myths and revelations.

7

Are Our Early Ideas about Divinity and Jesus Beneficial for Us? Yes, but Newer Ideas Are Needed.

This chapter is an invitation to reach out for a new discovery of God in our lives. A discovery is not reducible to a predefined bit of knowledge (belief). A discovery involves something new, different from a belief previously held. As an author, I have learned one thing: always respect a person's beliefs and discoveries because they are personal and important to that person. If you want someone to listen to what you have to say, you have to respect their faith experience as being topmost in their life. Though it may appear that I am a bit critical of certain traditional beliefs, the reality is quite the opposite. Most beliefs and discoveries about God should be valued because they show a unique personal experience of God.

I would like to share a personal insight about religious experiences. I have discovered that a new experience of the presence of God in my life is just as important for my faith as any traditional knowledge I may have of God. To illustrate this insight, I will now focus on the concepts of divinity and the Son of God. Perhaps they will become personalized and add something unique to your belief about God. Furthermore, I will also share with you why I think traditional ideas about divinity and Jesus Christ should be reexamined.

My early years were filled with traditional beliefs and practices. Several times a week, our entire family knelt on the living room floor and shared in the evening holy Rosary. Can you imagine doing this with your family today? My mother, a strict convert to the Catholic faith, was adamant that our spirituality mirror the important practices that filled her early days as a new Catholic. We frequented the confessional several times a month, holy Mass and Communion on Sundays, and we always attended a Catholic school. Out of these practices, I formed my early ideas about God, with all the trappings. As I mentioned in an earlier chapter, I formed initial images of God as an authoritarian figure, and as I grew in my faith, I arrived at my first discoveries of what God might be like. These discoveries arose out of an inquiry into the definitions I had learned in my early years. With those discoveries came my personal experience of the divine presence and the importance of God in my life.

A Starting Point on Divinity

Our search for God does not start from nothing. Our search usually begins with a multitude of treasured traditions and definitions given to us by our parents and teachers. From them, we learn ideas about what it means to be God, what it means to be divine, and what it means to be the Son of God. I have spent years pondering these three topics. However, please remember I am not trying to convince you of anything. I am merely sharing some insights important to me.

I have discovered that there is a definite evolution of thought on what it means to be God, starting with the Old Testament understanding and progressing into New Testament teachings. My early ideas about God were framed in beliefs passed on by people who lived under the influence of Greek and Roman traditions, as well as Jewish beliefs. The concept of Christ as God fits into my picture as a product of these many and varied traditions.

There is another insight I want to share with you in my search for God and Godlike experiences. It is this: most believers have received insights about God from an outside source. This is fortunate, since our education in life is from those who have cared for and instructed us in our movement toward maturity. As far as religion is concerned, there is no doubt the same process occurred for our parents, teachers, and others. What we need to be aware of is that most of what we have received came in the form of a statement about God, rather than as an invitation to discover the God experience from within. When we receive definitions of God and do not pursue the discovery aspect, we have done a disservice to our spiritual life. In most religious institutions, we find a continual defining process occurring. The reason is that believers are never satisfied with a particular definition of God, and religious institutions keep redefining God.

Occasionally, new doctrines and dogmas surface in the Christian church's history. However, we should remember that when we define something, we automatically put parameters around the subject defined. By doing this, we have limited, or at least restricted, our creative thinking on who God is. The Roman Catholic Church has a history of this practice. It has volumes of information classified as "De Fide Definita" statements. This means these statements are considered to be the absolute truth about matters relating to God and revelation: the case is closed.

When all the effort in religion is to define God, there is little room left for an experience of God as a discovery from within. During my early years as a seminarian, I was given definitions, then told to go and pray on them. That was it. There was no encouragement to seek a new insight. Dutifully, I did as I was told.

Can you spell out any doctrine about God that is satisfactory in all aspects? The answer should be a resounding *no*. We have received everything we know about God from the authority of people who lived and taught (preached) at a given time in the past, along with insights offered in the context of that specific time. We can say the same about how we received our original beliefs about Jesus, what He taught, and how preachers have defined Him to be Savior at a given time in history. This is understandable. Problems occur when Christian theologians declare some belief about God to be absolutely true and then write volumes of esoteric and fabricated statements in an attempt to show other Christians why what they say has to be absolutely correct. I believe matters of faith should always be open to scrutiny.

When I discuss Jesus and all the sacred mysteries surrounding our Savior, I freely use the same terminology that everyone else uses. For instance, the Son of God, miracles, resurrection, soul, afterlife—all have meaning for me now as a believer, and I treasure these items of beliefs as my own. My understanding of what these beliefs mean may not be the same as it is for others, but this is not as important as sharing with you that we value the same traditions passed on to us by our ancestors. I am not trying to convince you that I am correct about a spiritual belief, but I am inviting you to think a bit differently about spiritual matters and look at other ways of possibly expanding our discovery of God's presence in our lives.

My wife and I have discussed the topic of how many people do not want to be challenged with new insights into their religious beliefs. They exhibit an inherent hesitancy to move from a comfortable known into the mysterious unknown. Many acquaintances of ours have commented about my previous work, *The Evolution of Belief,* and how they found some parts "very interesting." My impression is that they did not want to be disturbed by having their traditional beliefs questioned. Some readers may think the same way about this book, as they are hesitant to look at some truths of faith in a different way. Perhaps there are more important things in their lives than discovering something new about God. This disturbs me. It indicates that people tend to cling to what supported their lives of faith when they were young, and do not want to allow into their faith any unsettling proposals about experiencing God in a new way.

Most of us want to live out our lives with a sense of peace. For the ordinary person, praying in the traditional way and looking for God in the tabernacle is a comfort zone. This is understandable. However, when we refuse to look at new possibilities and new ways of discovering God, the game is proverbially over. In my mind, clinging absolutely to a belief indicates a stagnant condition. As I mentioned before, the nature of a human mind is to continually look for something more fulfilling. An immovable position on a belief indicates a form of stoppage. While we are alive, we need to continually question and look for new discoveries and insights into the elements of our faith.

This next portion of the chapter on ideas about God reflects my own insight into what divinity could mean. At no time am I insisting that you accept what I have to say. I am simply sharing the processes I needed to work through to bring a sense of religious satisfaction into my life.

Humanity versus Divinity

To talk about our humanity as opposed to God's divinity is a good starting point. As knowledgeable people, we continually learn important things about humanity. Our learning on this issue is real and constantly evolving. However, the issue of divinity appears static and hinges on the authority of the ancients and the word of others in recent history. We know nothing about the divine nature of God, except what we have learned from someone else about an entity not existing in time. We believe that since our nature is inadequate to the task of reaching salvation, we need a redeemer, and that is God. Jesus is that human and divine component revealed to us, who can save us from something. I suggest we need to look more closely at divinity and what is revealed to us in the writings of the ancients.

What does it mean to be divine? I do not know, but I believe being divine in the traditional Christian sense is less meaningful to me today. Our ideas of divinity need to be constantly reexamined and hung up on the clothesline of faith with a new brilliance. I will explain why this is the case.

Old Testament Understanding of Divinity

Ancient Israelites had a very straightforward understanding of what God the Almighty meant: God is all-powerful, all knowing, and all benevolent. When they failed in obedience to God, there came the all-powerful vengeance and punishment. Divinity meant *not human* in nature, apart, and not at all sharing the human condition. Father McKenzie addresses some Hebrew writings about God and what they thought about His divine nature in ancient times:

> The existence of a divine being is never a problem in the Old Testament, and no discussion or demonstration is required. This conviction Israel shared with other peoples in the ancient Near East; the difference between Israel and these peoples turned on the identity of the divine being, not upon his reality and existence ... God is described as he who sits on the throne of Glory, in luminous brilliance, and this glorious king is the glorious God, the God-king of cloud and fire (His identity). This would be in reference to Psalm 29, 26, Is. 11:10, and many other references. This Old Testament concept is used by the synoptic writers (New Testament gospels) in the same fashion, where the brilliance of the glory of Jesus is manifested by anticipation in His transfiguration. The throne of the Glory of God is found in all the synoptic Gospels. This attribution illustrates the early believer's idea of God, and what it means to be divine. The identity of God is one that exhibits glorious characteristics, and these glorious characteristics are what makes God all powerful, all knowing, and all benevolent.[17]

For McKenzie, the reality of God and His existence was a given in the Old Testament. It is as if the Hebrews proclaimed a God before they knew many details about what that meant. God's characteristics later became important topics of conversation. There were many conversations between man and God in the Old Testament, to the point that it was difficult to tell the difference between the ancient Hebrews speaking and God speaking. This is particularly noted during the conquest of the Promised Land. However, the difference between God and man was how God was identified. There was no question about His existence, as all other nations believed in the reality and existence of a God as well.

Separating the idea of God and His identity was paramount in order to show that the Hebrew God (the highest of all gods) was not like the pagan gods of the time.

Looking at divinity in general, we can say that the idea of God meant different things to different religious believers over time. Each religion has modified the use and understanding of what it means to be divine. The religious institution develops its understanding of how a deity can fit in with the context of the time. Christianity is no different. Furthermore, once we have accumulated many believers whose adherence to a leader's convictions is firm, then a faithful mind will accommodate itself to anything, even though it might be beyond reason.

Humankind is constantly looking for answers to the finiteness of the world. If there is a God, the default would be the acceptance of some creative entity that is everlasting and powerful, and this belief would necessarily accommodate many irrational and presumptive beliefs. With such thinking, we could see why, if creation means begetting something from nothing, then there would be a conclusion that a super powerful (divine entity) brought this world into existence. If matter is finite, then a conclusion would be to attribute the source of materiality to an immaterial entity, which, of course would be a divine entity. These are just two of many attempts to define the identity of a God already acknowledged to exist. A problem arises here. God is a distinct entity (out there) instead of being a presence, a divine presence, with us now.

The ideas of creation out of nothingness, and the source of the finite being an immaterial entity, is a good starting point for a discussion. There is no proof that matter is eternal. So also, there is no proof that matter is finite and had to have been created, in the sense of being created out of nothing. The idea of creation in the traditional sense falters, just as the ideas proposed by the Flat Earth Society fall flat. We simply cannot prove it. We just believe it. Divinity, or God, in the Judeo-Christian tradition, always implies the "author of creation." This, of course, means the creation of something from nothing. The false premises behind such thinking will lead to false conclusions. Occasionally, lapses in rational thinking occur because there is an innate need to explain the cause of something.

Theologians and philosophers have always attributed the source of creation to an uncreated source or primal and first cause (a philosophical term), which source would have to be infinite. They reason that if something is finite, then it must have been created by an infinite source. Hence, the traditional understanding of a God is one who is infinite. This is another contribution to what we know as being divine. The only way I can put closure to the discussion on the identity of God is to say we know nothing about immateriality and creation out of nothing. We only know the myths and superstitions from which we draw conclusions.

I admit traditional beliefs have supported our faith for centuries. In addition, we might feel the presence of God, but we cannot possibly grasp what all knowing, all-powerful, and all benevolent might mean (even today, we confuse *all benevolent* with *all provident*). The ancients could only use the thoughts available at the time for understanding God. Are we strapped to the ancients' way of thinking? We do not have to be. The identity of God could be just a simple and enduring presence in our lives.

As discussed earlier, we live in an A to B world and are limited to a space-time structure. Divinity, infinity, eternity, and creation (in the traditional sense of the words) are not within our comprehension. We can only speculate on what these terms might mean because we know our own boundaries and limitations. I would like to carry this discussion further, using the traditional ideas about the Son of God.

What Is Meant by the Son of God?

When it comes to understanding the meaning of Son of God in Hebrew belief, the ideas are straightforward. The Son of God concept among the Hebrews and early Christians was not about the existence of demigods, as found in Hellenistic (Greek) religious beliefs. Demigods represented the incarnation of an individual produced by a Greek god mating with a human. This incarnated individual had some characteristics of a god (in Greek, Zeus, or among the Romans, Jupiter) yet possessed some behaviors of humankind.

The ancient Hebrew understanding of Son of God was not that of an individual with both divine and human qualities but rather a human who is chosen, who has a mission, and who is usually a prophet, leading the people to walk in the ways of God's commands. At that time, to think otherwise would be to succumb to the pagan beliefs in Mesopotamia (the place of the Israelite exile) and, later on, to the influence of Greek mythology. To be sons and daughters of God, in Hebrew belief, was to be a people and/or a person who recognized the identity of the one God (monotheism) who was truly glorious. Even at the time of Jesus, many Jews viewed the concept of being the sons and daughters of God as being human. Israel is even referred to as the sons and daughters of God. The use of Son of God in the Old Testament never meant being divine (having glorious power).

The Son of Man in the New Testament appears more than eighty times as a saying by Jesus in St. John and the Synoptic Gospels, and there is a controversy over the possibility these were textual alterations to show early believers that Jesus was truly human as well as God. The question now centers on what is meant by Son of God in the New Testament literature. Does the Son of God necessarily mean an individual possessing divine qualities?

Most New Testament writers believed that Jesus possessed qualities of a divine nature. St John has Jesus telling the disciples about God His Father. The Jews seem to have heard that idea when they accused Jesus of blasphemy and tried to stone Him to death. The incidents revealing the powers of God in the person of Jesus were many, with the Jews witnessing many miracles unheard of before. Testimonies by Peter, Thomas, and possibly by the other apostles, at least indicated that Jesus was not just a special rabbi who preached the good news but that He possessed qualities of the Lord God Almighty. After all, Jesus worked an abundance of miracles. St. Paul waxes eloquently about this belief in his letter to the Philippians when he says Jesus is equal in glory with the Father.

The early fathers of the church were clear in their statements about the divinity of Jesus being like the divinity of the Father. Ignatius of Antioch (110 CE), Clement (190 CE), Gregory the Wonderworker (265 CE), and many others proclaimed Jesus was part of the Godhead and, although human, was indeed God. St. Irenaeus, in his letter *Against Heresies* 1:10:1 (189 CE), described, in simple creed form, the divine nature of Jesus as equal to the Father and Holy Spirit.[18]

In New Testament times, there was an awareness of Hellenic (Greek) influence, which led Christians to insist that the Son of God was not like a demigod. The Christian God is all-powerful, all knowing, and all benevolent, and His Son participates in the

Godhead; He is not a frail offspring of a God mating with a human. The early fathers of the church insisted that Jesus was fully God and fully man at the same time. The challenge for a Christian believer today is to make sense of a God-man in the person of Jesus versus the ancient Hebrew idea of what Son of God meant.

Given all this information about Jesus as pictured for us in early Christian literature, what is it that we can carry forward into the future? If the ancient Israelites and early Christians thought of divinity as being a glorious condition that humans could not attain, what can we say and believe about Jesus today? A description of God as being glorious, which permeates the Old Testament, involves God's power, which all should fear, because God is a vengeful God who demands obedience to His commands. This belief does not appear to align well with the early Christians' practice of compassion, forgiveness, and brotherly love for all peoples (the good news). The new idea of being saved by the death and resurrection of Jesus was preached by St. Paul. Is this belief of being saved by the coming of Jesus adequate for what we need to carry into our own time and into the future? I do not think so. According to St. Paul, Jesus had to be divine, because we are fallen and necessarily had to be saved by a divine entity. However, we are not fallen angels but risen primates. St. Paul did not know this. He only knew in faith what he had been taught. He was taught that Adam and Eve, our first parents, had fallen from innocence and grace.

The concept of being saved needs to be changed today. Being born in sin and needing to be saved does not resonate with modern inquiring minds. The Israelites were always punished by a vindictive God when they disobeyed His commandments. Later on, the prophetic preaching of the Jews led the early Christians to proclaim Jesus as the promised Messiah. Consequently, the beliefs about the promised Messiah and the supposed saving actions of Jesus are what held the early community together.

Just as descriptions about the Hebrew God pointed to a God unlike the Mesopotamian gods (making the Hebrew people a special people), so also Jesus became the fulfillment figure promised in Jewish history, when the nation of Israel would once again find its place in the world under the one and holy God. The problem is that, following Christian doctrine, Jesus did not come to restore the nation of Israel but to bring the good news of His father to the entire world, and He died in the process.

I invite you to look at divinity and Son of God from another perspective. Given the ancient beliefs about God as a being glorious on His throne, and early Christian thought about Jesus being divine and equal to the Father, we need to rediscover what these concepts might mean for us today. The idea of God for us today can be all of what tradition has given us, because we need to treasure those ideas as discoveries offered to us as our faith continues to develop. However, we cannot stop at this point and say, "There it is," and be satisfied. I believe there is a need for more discoveries and quests for a continued growth.

In my quest for a deeper understanding about God, I had to revisit and critically look at the basis for traditional ideas and what it may mean for the contemporary believer today. For more than two thousand years, Christians have been praying over the traditional idea about the divinity of Christ as proposed by countless theologians. The traditional attributes of God had to be included in the understanding of what the divinity of Christ means. We oftentimes forget that what we mean by Christ being a gift to us is contextual (time dependent).

Since early times, divinity has remained a stagnant concept in that we cannot do anything with it. We really do not know what divinity means. Our traditional belief tells us that Christ absolutely had to rise again from the dead in a glorified body in order to save us from our sinful nature. For a resurrection to occur, there had to have been a divine intervention of some kind. The Son of God was the recipient of the intervention of God the Father, and therefore Christ must share in what it means to be all-powerful, all knowing, all benevolent. Other than what we might believe in faith, we simply cannot comprehend what the divinity of Christ means.

Instead of carrying out the Hebrew tradition of Son of God, the early Christians preached a different theology and not the earlier belief, which preached that sons and daughters of God were such by virtue of communicating the word of God to a chosen people.[19] Within a few decades, there was a theological shift within the Christian community. We may never know why this occurred, but the Jewish diaspora, the early Christian community, and St. Paul's preaching had a major part to play in this theological shift.

I believe we need to move from the saving aspect of Jesus toward a response to an invitation to live out the good news of Jesus Christ. The theology of salvation now becomes an invitation to live out the good news, which allows Jesus to rise again in the world through our good actions.

The purpose of discussing the Son of God issue is an attempt on my part to connect the ancient Hebrew concept with the meaning of the modern Christian idea of being sons and daughters of God. The gift of being a son and daughter of God comes with being able to share the goodness and importance of God in one's life today. This is an ongoing process and is never complete but rather always somewhat unfulfilled (this topic is treated in more detail in a later chapter).

Rather than looking at divinity from the point of view of an entity that can save the fallen nature of humans, we can now look at understanding the divinity of Jesus as arising from the promotion of the good news spread by the sons and daughters of God in the present. This allows us to look at Jesus's divinity from a more reasonable perspective. We are the body of Christ present in the world by our witness to the good news. Although at times we may be selfish and evil, we cannot be in need of a Savior simply because of an outdated idea about Adam, Eve, and original sin.

Would it be too brazen to say that Jesus's divinity could be thought of in a different way? Instead of being described in terms of a God who came to save us (the traditional understanding), why not apply the ancient Israelite idea of the son of God as one chosen, set apart, called to witness the good news of God? In this view, Jesus would not be divine but uncommonly human, an extraordinary person whose personhood we truly need to reflect in our lives. Jesus was the ultimate Godlike person spoken of earlier in chapter 3. We have no idea of what divinity is, other than our human-made notions of the qualities of God. We only know that humans are not equal to those qualities. I believe it unnecessary to pin these perceived qualities of God onto the personality of Jesus.

If we reflect the kingdom of the Father in our hearts and lives, would our devotion to Jesus really change that much? When we share the bread and cup at liturgies, would we not still be in communion with one another, as indeed we are the body of Christ for the world? We are the only way Jesus can be present as a Savior for humanity. Jesus does not walk our paths from town to town the way He did in Palestine. By virtue of being baptized as Christians, we become Jesus for people. We are the ones expected to walk in His ways. It is through our good actions that Jesus is able to be risen from the dead. On our part, we can experience a resurrection of Jesus every day of our lives.

Now all the ideas about Jesus we have accepted in the past can be discovered and nurtured in a new way. I am not taking anything important away from Jesus. I am putting a new light on our importance as witnesses to a different understanding of how the resurrection of Christ took place and how it takes place in today's world. Jesus is the Son of God constantly rising from the dead in the bodies of Christians who share the good news of the Father. This would be a serious invitation to us, rather than an unexplained need to be redeemed.

In conclusion, I believe we need to move ahead with new insights that can accommodate to the world in which we live. We simply cannot live in a world of thoughts and proclamations that tied down a certain belief two or three thousand years ago. In today's world, the traditional God qualities and the nature of a divine entity fall short as we move ahead in our search for God. We need to let the divine presence speak to us in the context of our own times. Past definitions will never be understood completely today. I find my proposal about the Son of God and His divinity credible. I also I admit there will always be a quest to understand more about Jesus, the Son of God.

At this time, I believe we need to relinquish many early ideas about something coming from nothing and Jesus having to be divine in the traditional sense. We need to move forward with new discoveries about the meaning of the kingdom of God in our hearts today, in today's world. We can treasure many traditional ideas as valuable in themselves, the way we might treasure ancient dinnerplates, careful to never place today's dinner on these artifacts. We need new wineskins to hold what we deem precious to drink at this time. I view it as being in one place, then having traveled all the way around the world, seeing the original place as something new and different, enriching and satisfying my heart in a new way.

My invitation is, "We can do this." We can let the kingdom of God in our hearts be what is eternal, all-powerful, all knowing, and all benevolent. We can release ourselves from old arguments about the nature of a divinity and proclamations asserting Jesus as being both God and man. We can then just let the Spirit (the divine presence) be within us, as we know deep down it has always been there.

8

Are There Other Religions That Offer Eternal Salvation? Yes.

At this point, it is important to look at religion as a whole. This chapter's intent is to show there are many ways to learn and continue a search for God. However, some religions are better at satisfying our ideas about God than others. Cultures and traditional practices around the world overlap into the domain of religious belief. Often it is difficult to separate out traditional cultural practices from essential religious beliefs. We sometimes miss an essential search for God in certain religions because of some distasteful cultural practices intertwined with a genuine and valid religious belief. The discussion about how religions offer knowledge and eternal salvation when worshiping a God is interesting but somewhat complicated. I will attempt to simplify my ideas as I offer my thoughts on the matter.

I live within a multicultural community and have had many discussions on what traditional religious thought has done to stir up discontent around the world. One belief that sows discontent is the teaching that "I am right, and God is on my side." Religious adherents have brought many terrible things upon humanity because of the erroneous belief that they alone possess the truth, and since God is on their side, they are justified in promoting immoral and even barbaric practices.

A related belief is that there is no salvation outside a given religion. The Roman Catholic Church is guilty of this belief, which excludes all religions not centered on the saving actions of Jesus Christ. The Inquisitions in Europe were just one terrible example of "God being on my side." This belief is not exclusive to Christianity. Islam also considers all nonbelievers as infidels needing to be eradicated.[20] Ancient Israel had similar beliefs, and we read in the Pentateuch about practices of exterminating pagans.[21] Whose side is God on anyway? I cite Western religions here, as most of my readers (although not all) originate from a Greco-Roman tradition, but other religions are guilty of this as well.

I coached football in Catholic high schools for most of my thirty-four-year teaching career. On the day of a game, my team attended morning Mass before classes. Just before kickoff, we would say a prayer in a large huddle and end with a resounding "Amen" and the name of our team. However, at no time did I think God was on our side. I did believe that victory could be ours if we were up for the game, played as a close-knit team, and encouraged one another through all four quarters. Mass and prayer were more about being together and achieving a pregame winning attitude. This was more important to me than the actual outcome of the game. Simply being together as a unit, we became something greater than the sum total of the parts. We were actually a winning team; we were empowered, and at Saint Francis High School, we won nearly all of our games. But enough of tipping my own hat. My point is that I believe God is on everyone's side. Because I am a sports enthusiast, I use the sport of football as an analogy of religious thought about God being on one side rather than on another.

Many forget that although theological tenets persist, religious practices, rituals, and ceremonies are time dependent and change over time. Because I am Christian, I know that although Christian practices can change over time, theological tenets may not change and instead hang on for many centuries. However, it is through the genuine religious faith of an individual or community, not theological tenets, that the presence of God empowers the believer. As an example, the presence of God enters into the body of Christ (the believing community) through rituals and ceremonies. I want to show that there are many practices (not tenets) that can facilitate the coming of a divine presence into a believing community.

Initially, we need to work from a framework of belief for arriving at some type of understanding and appreciation of a divinity. I believe varied cultures and religious beliefs can be valid ways of moving toward a discovery of God in our lives. From my adolescent years, I was instructed that although Christ has redeemed the world, there is no salvation outside the Catholic Church. This proclamation is seriously mistaken. The church still preaches this extraordinary, exclusive, and overpowering control over divine presence. Such beliefs lead to the conviction that most of the people in the world will go to hell if they are not baptized in the Catholic Church. The Catholic Church is really saying that the billions of immortal souls practicing Hinduism, Islam, Judaism, and a variety of other religious beliefs are destined to be lost forever. These souls do not have access to the saving graces of Christ without the church. However, Christ is supposed to have lived and died for all of humanity. The position of the Catholic Church on this matter, along with many other Christian churches, is very questionable, and in the following paragraphs, I will attempt to explain why this is the case.

As Christians search for God, eventually they will discover that the belief that God is on their side is an aberration and represents a false teaching. I remember asking my mother, when two Catholic football teams are competing, how does God choose who will be the winner, and what is the process by which God makes this decision? My mother replied that the decision is up to God and "That is the way things are. Do not argue about it." I mentioned earlier that God is on everyone's side. He does not play favorites with any of His children, Christian or non-Christian. To the present day, I live by my opinion, and I have been able to solve this type of dilemma quickly. In the matter of sports, the correct answer is that the better and smarter team wins.

From our youngest years, Christians have been educated with a set of convictions that the saving nature of God's power comes from the teachings of Jesus Christ. These teachings have been so ingrained in our psyches that there is no room for any other way of looking at God, except through the Western Judeo-Christian perspective. I am not saying this is an unfortunate position. What I am saying is that we have learned about God in a particular and contextual framework. When our religious education was taking place, there was no room for any other religion. This is not a bad thing altogether, since it can solidify and empower a religious community. However, we must remember there are other cultures and religions existing around the world that do not worship within a Christian context but still have, as a religious system, the practice of searching for God.

We need to admit that other religions actually do search for and discover God in their own way. We should respect this and not be obstinate in our convictions about salvation only being attained through Jesus Christ. There is nothing unusual about multiple beliefs. They exist. That there are other cultures exercising a quest for ultimate fulfillment in a divinity is good and indicates that deep within the human psyche is a drive for fulfilment in a God belief. The evolution of multiple belief systems takes place in much the same way in all societies, civilizations, organizations, and populations that have existed in history. The fact that there are different religions in the world shows how important time, culture, and circumstances are to an integral part of the discovery of God in our lives.

A problem arises when the Roman Catholic Church declares itself to be the sole arbiter of what God wants us to do. In other words, the will of God is defined by the church. Egregious things have happened in history under the guise of the church's claim to be the dispenser of God's will. This type of proclamation leaves no room for any other discovery or quest for understanding God's presence and will for us.

As far as the Christian experience is concerned, we should never devalue traditional beliefs and stories that are meaningful, as long as they are not harmful. They are important for putting color and spiritual life into our daily quest for discovering God. We need to treasure them as important building blocks for our faith in God, and we should never toss them away as meaningless stories and myths. They are important for us because they form part of our innate experience of God.

When we call out in our hearts for the source of our fulfillment, we necessarily call out and make use of the source of our learned experience of God. Deep within my psyche is etched a quantum of religious belief. By this I mean my heart will always turn soft to a religious song sung well (such as "Amazing Grace"), a prayer, or meaningful and modest laying on of hands at a religious event. As a Christian, I may have a different understanding of what the

Eucharist means, but the attachment and need is still there to participate in the body of Christ. To be part of the body of Christ will always be a Christian's yearning, never to go away. Other religions have a similar experience. We need to respect this fact.

I am sure there is a longing that other religions have in searching for a divine presence in their communities. All traditions are part of the human psyche, regardless of the place and time in human history. Each belief is part of an individual's experience of God as a believer moves on to final fulfillment. But it is important to separate valid religious experiences from discriminatory cultural practices.

A good way of sorting out erroneous beliefs is to measure them against the early Hebrew injunction of doing unto to others as you would have them do unto you. If the practice does not measure up to this standard, then it is not part of a bundle of experiences leading to a further discovery of God, regardless of where it is in the world and in what religion people might worship. It is important to remember that our beliefs are not a final understanding about God but only a snapshot in our religious experience as we discover God. They are a temporary snapshot because the quest for total fulfillment in God always looks ahead.

Circumcision and Defining a Religion

When I was a coach, on game day, everyone on the team wore a game jersey, even the managers. That day, the kids were special and set apart, and they competed on behalf of the school. Our team was a special group, and each player had a part to play. The jerseys stood out in the hallways and were worn with pride. This sense of belonging generates the same power and effect in religious communities as it does in football.

When it comes to a group proclamation of an understanding of God, we accept the religious laws and practices of that believing group. As an example, the Israelites proclaimed God through a common ritual that identified the participants as different, set apart, and special. In the Hebrew religion there was the practice of circumcision of all male young adults. The law of circumcision appears in Genesis 17:10 ff, and it is a part of the covenant of God with Abraham. All males born in the household of Abraham, whether free or slave, were to be circumcised eight days after birth. All adult male converts were to be circumcised immediately. This obligation was serious, and failure to fulfill it meant separation from the covenant (Genesis17:14). The practice of circumcision appears throughout the entire Old Testament as a sign of membership in the Hebrew religion and its covenant with God.[22] This covenant regulation was an ideal way to prove membership in Israel at any given time in its history, especially when conflicts with the pagans were frequent. In Hebrew history, adherence to the covenant ritual was the form of a guarantee of divine presence, primitive as this ritual might be.

After the resurrection of Jesus, the regulation for males to be circumcised was dropped for non-Jewish Christians (Gentiles) and was not considered an absolute requirement under the new covenant. However, the practice is still widespread among the Jewish, Islamic, and some Christian sects even to this day. The high incidence of circumcision today may be tied to present-day cultural traditions rather than to the persistence of an ancient Hebrew covenant. The point I wish to make here is that Judeo-Christian and Islamic religions have followed certain regulations in order for their followers to be recipients of the blessings promised as part of a covenant relationship. Religious practices and rituals do change with the times, but the faith of the community persists.

Death to All outside a Covenant Relationship

Having looked at the difference between ancient practices and a genuine faith response to the presence of God in a community, I wish to discuss now how some faulty theological principles arose from an absolute adherence to the demands of the one true God. Remember, for the Hebrews, the existence of God was not a question. God's identity continued to be explored by the early leaders on behalf of the Hebrew community.

Among most religious groups, especially in the Judeo-Christian tradition, there is a requirement to adhere to the rules and regulations of the members of a group. With the Hebrews, an agreement to adhere to certain conditions is called a covenant. Adherence to the rules was often so strict that failure was punishable by death. As an example, we have the belief of the Hebrews with regard to the takeover of the Promised Land. After being homeless more than four hundred years in Egypt, and an additional forty years wandering in the desert, the Hebrews thought of Palestine as their land for establishing the kingdom of Israel. They believed that as long as they adhered to all the aspects of a covenant relationship, they would get their promised land. In accordance with the covenant, any objectors to the takeover were to be killed, banished, or became slaves to the conquering tribes of Israel.

Another example is the documented accounts of baptism, followed by the execution of natives in the Americas by Christian Spanish conquistadors. Furthermore, all sorts of examples of mass execution have occurred, even in modern times in parts of Africa, because of religious differences. It is true that some massacres took place as the result of opposing cultural/ethnic ideologies, but many such instances are those that carry deep religious differences.

Throughout the Torah and the Koran, those who refused to become Hebrew and Muslim were always described as infidels, worthy of banishment and/or death. This becomes problematic when we consider searching for a God experience in a different belief or practice. To arrive at any kind of peace during such conflicts, there has to have been an accommodation to and relaxation of some of these religious demands. This actually did happen in the resolution to the covenant that required circumcision when there was a transition from Jewish traditions into early Christian times. Accommodation by Muslims also occurred as Islam spread throughout the Middle East after the fall of the Roman Empire.

No Salvation outside a Covenant Relationship

Today, rigid enforcement of covenants takes the form of a declarative position rather than a physical confrontation. Statements surface from the heads of religious groups declaring that there is no salvation outside their church, mosque, or synagogue. As much as we believe such thinking is idiotic and stupid, it is endemic. Such declarations are still formalized and preached in holy places. They occur within the Catholic Church. For instance, as a Catholic, if your child was not baptized, the church stated that he/she would not enter into heaven. The church would not say that your unbaptized child would go to hell but possibly to a place called Limbo. There was no complete salvation without receiving the sacrament of baptism.

It was not until April 2007 that a commission of Catholic theologians, under the authority of Pope Benedict XVI, declared that babies who died before being baptized would no longer be trapped in Limbo. Just where they must spend eternity is not clear, only that it would not be in hell. The Vatican thought that God would not be so cruel as to condemn unbaptized children to the flames of hell. God was loving and compassionate to the "little ones." This declaration represents a definite softening of the church's understanding since the time of St. Augustine. Augustine was insistent that unbaptized children must necessarily suffer the consequence of eternal punishment.[23]

We are witnessing new answers to questions, not about the existence of God but what God is like and what we think God expects of us (His identity). This whole problem arose from a system of beliefs entrenched in a false supposition that man is fallen in nature. Because of original sin, the only way to be saved is to be baptized in the name of Jesus. The problem is still not solved.

Instead of searching for God, the church defines the nature of God, using somewhat unfounded presumptions handed down over the centuries. But it is unfortunate to have dogmas and doctrines that are based on myths with morals, rather than being based on a reasonable stance. We cannot take time-dated writings literally. From an onlooker's point of view, throughout the history of the Christian church, there has been a constant backpedaling. This represents a good example of a specific religious institution, such as the Catholic Church, defining God by man-made declarations, rather than emphasizing a search for God. Hopefully, it will not be long before additional changes will occur, including statements that all good individuals can be admitted into the heavenly kingdom, even if they are unbaptized.

Traditional thought maintains that the Adam and Eve episode had to be a historical event, because we are sinful and need of salvation through Jesus Christ, who suffered and died for us so that we could be saved. We are born in a state of sin, and Jesus, through His death and resurrection, is the only one who can save us. To be saved, we must be in a covenant relationship with God the Father. In this scenario, there is no allowance for humankind's evolution into human consciousness from the lower primates. Instead of there being a search for God in our lives, there is adherence to a set of doctrines and dogmas put in place by prelates and theologians who structured a system of thought mandated for all to believe. Because of sin, there is physical and spiritual death. Only by adherence to the early Christian beliefs can we determine our position with God. There is no other way out for anybody. There is no other way to reach fulfillment in God's presence. The Christian church, as a group, defines God and, in that effort, excludes all other peoples and religions from a saving presence outside the scope of its own belief.

What Salvation in Other Religions Could Mean

As a Catholic, denial of salvation for nonbelievers has always been a thorn in my side. The belief that salvation can only be achieved through acceptance of Jesus Christ, who redeemed the whole of humanity (in the past and in the future), was constantly on my mind, much like a puzzle unable to be put together. The Christian church has been, for two thousand years, a missionary entity bent on saving those who are not yet saved. The problem is that the Christian church is not getting any closer to saving the world by the redeeming power of Christ than it was back in the first century. Although a major religion in the world, the vast majority of humankind is not Christian, not to mention those who are Christian in name only and do not practice a Christian faith at all. For many Christians, baptism, marriage, and burial services are relegated to the level of cultural practices.

When observing other religions and their ideas of eternal salvation, we see no consistent demand for conversion. With the exception of religions stemming from the Abrahamic tradition

(Judaism, Christianity, and Islam), acceptance into a "saved community" is more cultural than religious. But within the Judeo-Christian framework, we have religious institutions defining what God is like and what He demands, rather than exploring a spiritual experience of discovering God. Obligatory statements originating from revelation are examples of the most irrational statements ever applied to something Christ said or did not say.

Far Eastern religions carry less absolute adherence to a specific way of belief than the Western religions. The beliefs that espouse reincarnation narratives indicate no eternal salvation until a soul is purified in some way. The consequence of not being ready for eternal bliss would be to reenter life as another person or animal of some kind. Furthermore, most Eastern religions define salvation as a merger with an absolute or god (multiple gods and lesser gods). Resurrection of the body is unimportant, since escaping from the body is the major objective of the believer. Below is a synopsis of some critical beliefs of several major world religions.

Hinduism: Salvation means to be liberated from earthly desire by deepening a relationship with a god or many gods. This is achieved through love and knowledge of God. Brahma is the highest force and cause of all that exists. A soul (spiritual entity) must allow God to enfold it in such a way that it is carried away from a mortal existence. Reincarnation is the default if God perceives the soul is not ready for immortality.

Buddhism: This religion preaches that its followers should strive to be released totally from earthly desires. Suffering stops when one does not desire any material things. Life is a cycle of suffering and rebirth. It is possible to escape this cycle when the spirit is totally liberated from anything material. Siddhartha Gautama (the Buddha) is believed to have reached this state called nirvana. Salvation is not an issue since modern-day Buddhism does not adhere to the necessity of any required deity to reach nirvana, the goal of all its followers.

Taoism: In history, this Eastern religion at one time believed in physical as well as spiritual immortality, but the physical aspects of immortal human existence have been discarded in favor of one's spirit flowing perfectly with nature, where there is no distinction between life and death. This form of religious belief results in salvation, which, to its proponents, is unexplainable.

Monotheism: The belief in one true God includes the Hebrew patriarchal religions: Judaism, Christianity, and Islam. These three major religions of the Western world view the afterlife and salvation as a liberation from sin and establishing a personal relationship (covenant) with the one God. This God is creator and above all other gods. Included in the monotheistic belief are many other small and localized religions, all of which proclaim one Supreme Being. Ancient polytheistic religions of the Middle East, along with most religions, practiced manipulation and placation. This form of bribery is found in all three major monotheistic religions even to this day.

Judaism: In Judaism, in order to placate the monotheistic God, innocent animals were sacrificed so that humankind could be cleansed, and a lasting relationship with God could once again be secured. The Jewish faith is monotheistic, although not all its believers maintain adherence to an immortality and eternal place in heaven.

Christianity: To be a follower of Christ, the soul has to be saved in order to achieve eternal life. In the Roman Catholic Church, the believers are redeemed but need to work out their salvation. Fasting, keeping God's commandments, and doing good deeds are required, but it is by the saving actions of Jesus Christ that we are to have eternal life with God. Repentance and conversion (change of heart) are indicators that the saving actions of Christ are taking effect.

Islam: Everyone is a sinner, and you can only be saved by observing the five pillars of Islam—that is, prayer, fasting, almsgiving, a Hajj to Mecca, and absolute submission to Allah. Muslims can only hope that their good deeds will outweigh their bad deeds. The eternal life is a paradise where one can enjoy material and sensual things. In the end, it is Allah who decides heaven (a place where) and hell for humankind. Martyrdom is the only absolute way of sure salvation.

There are many other distinct religions spread across the world, with a variety of sects coming into existence and then fading away. Most religions express and teach absolute adherence to the commands of a deity. Some of these groups preach the immanence of God in everything, while others dictate the existence of a supreme being out and away from the material things of the earth. Religious believers generally declare the importance of a search for more meaning in their lives. Although seen to be false by a Christian believer, certain proclamations of other beliefs ought to be valued as attempts to find meaning in the world. The belief in a God and the understanding of eternity evolves over the centuries, but as long as one continues a search, the divine presence is there for all peoples. There are many ways to God, and although the idea of God does not change for most people, what eternity might mean always changes somewhat, as each discovery leads to a further quest for fulfillment.

On another point, it is important to note that the believer is the crucial component in the discovery of a deity, not an organized institution. If we remember in St. Mark's Gospel, the disciples came up to Jesus and complained about some people performing miracles in the name of Jesus. These people were not formal followers with the group of the disciples. Jesus rebuked the apostles and said that they should let these people be, because they were doing good things in His name. There is power within the heart when it proclaims the name of a deity. It does not matter if the name is Jesus, Mohamed, Allah, the gods of Hinduism, or any other religion. There is within all hearts the power to bring about good, regardless of the religious affiliation. Anyone can participate in the saving works by calling on the name of their deity. Salvation is there for people of all creeds when the love of others is the motive behind their actions.

We find in the evolution of religious beliefs a continual movement bent on acquiring more believers into the fold. The larger the mass of believers, the more powerful and persuasive the group becomes. The belief that a specific religion is the one and only source of God's direction implies another hidden motive, such as power or influence. The acquiring of numbers represents a greater potential for influence in the world. At all times in history, politics and military prowess have appeared to be the vehicles for a dominating religious belief. Most religious beliefs proclaiming eternal life and happiness are an attractive carrot for people wanting to believe in something and, at the same time, reap the benefits of a strong protector.

In conclusion, there appears to be a constant drive for most religious groups to define a deity rather than continue an effort to invite followers to a discovery and experience a deity. Defining a religious belief is critical for our understanding and ability to communicate with others about a belief in God. However, we cannot stop and be satisfied with just a definition. There is a constant need to rediscover what a particular belief means, and, of course, this always involves a search, a quest for fulfillment. All religions are on a path of discovery and for the most part are valid vehicles for recognizing a divine presence. Although not all cultural practices are equal and acceptable, there is a need to respect most beliefs as avenues to discovering God. We should always look for a bright side of truth in most religious beliefs. In some form, truth will always be there. We need to continue looking for it.

My intent has been to show that statements about God and declarations formulated as some form of exclusive revelation often take precedence over a sense of discovery. Since I am a Christian, I chose to focus on Christian doctrines and beliefs arising out of some assorted revelations. Most readers are likely Christians who search for a greater experience of God through a given revelation. Certainly, within traditional Christianity, this is the case. In Eastern religions, this appears to be less important, as is the case with religions such as Hinduism, Buddhism, and Taoism.

There are fewer defined proclamations in the Far Eastern religions, unlike the Christian dogmas and statements upheld as certain and unerring. In many Eastern religions, emphasis is placed upon a personal discovery of gods who are to be revered because they are wise and enjoy eternal life. We notice definite steps to fulfillment through a meditative process, but these are not absolute and obligatory. Failure to comply does not always involve damnation in Eastern religions but may lead to serious discriminative practices among localized populations.

Most devotional practices are precious and important for preserving an idea about God, even if that deity is not clearly defined. The achievement of peace and tranquility should be the hallmark of any discovery and quest for final fulfillment. If a quest in any religion does not bring about a more fulfilling peace, then it would be beneficial to take refuge in the confidence and assurance of another religious allegiance.

9

Can Any Discovery about God Allow Us to Continue Our Search? It Should.

You will notice that in most chapters of this book, I address sensitive religious issues in the first person. This is so because what I am saying is from me and about my own personal thoughts on a given topic; at no time am I implying that you should adopt what I say as the truth, but rather as something of interest and worth thinking about. In this chapter, I hope to relay my own personal religious experience in a simple and straightforward manner. The important strategy for me, in my search for God, was to examine carefully any new discovery in my religious experience. Having used definition as a starting point, my spiritual journey often entailed an initial quasi-rejection of that definition received earlier in life. However, I always seemed to arrive at the same concept again but with a different understanding.

An important component of the quest for more understanding of God is expectation. Expectation plays a critical role in moving a faith experience into a form of fulfillment. Such an attitude is always open to some kind of answer in my search and makes me confident that I will discover something new. It is more than relying on something to happen before I can proceed (like flipping a light switch before entering a lighted room). Expectation

fuels a quest for fulfillment when one is on a
some examples with which most people are far
something new about God does not stop the
need to continue on, expecting that something new and
will come about. Bear with me as I share some topics to show what
a religious discovery could accomplish.

Taking Another Look at the Necessary Qualities of a God

As one of the examples of discovery leading to an expectation, I would like to mention the discovery of the qualities of a deity treated in chapter 7. This is the discovery of a God who is all knowing, all-powerful, and all good, even in the face of the numerous disasters happening in our world. Remember, my awareness first started with a defined concept of God as given to me by my parents. It then morphed into a discovery that God was much more subtle than He appeared to be in my adolescent years. Having looked at my discovery about God with these three qualities, I considered what was happening in this process and what could be learned with this discovered insight. First, if God is all good, and I see a good deal of pain and suffering occurring in the world, what would I expect to do with this apparent contradiction?

The important thing here is not the insight so much as what I am doing with the insight. Given a sincere faith in God, I am expecting some form of answer to follow. As important as the answering of questions might be, just as important is the discovering that there are always more questions to be answered.

Expectation is the key element in this process of finding a mature and developing relationship with God in my life. I expect an answer to apparent contradictions or conundrums. An example would be: how could God be all good and allow so many bad

...ings to happen to so many people? This is an apparent contradiction, and I expect an answer to it. The expectation experience is absolutely important and crucial to me. If God exists and is present to me in the here and now, I expect some form of answer. I cannot just let this question die on the vine. I personally need to look at the problem here, as opposed to those who arrive at this contradiction and then just end the process. As it so happens, a good portion of educated and lapsed believers see contradictions such as this as an obstacle to experiencing any further acceptance of God. A loving God and calamity do not go well together.

It seems contradictory to think of a God who creates a world full of tragedy and yet is supposed to be all loving. It implies God must not be all loving in the first place. If He knew and had the power to prevent horrible calamities from happening in the world, then He would have done something about it. This is where we put real faith to the test. I expect that an answer will be discovered, or I would have to say that this situation is unexplainable and let my journey of faith stop. Being satisfied with saying, "This is how God works," and that "God has something planned," is not enough. I need to continue my quest. Expectation is essential. It is the impetus for learning more about my relationship with God. Although expectation does not always lead to something satisfactory, it will lead to something deeper and more rewarding. Stumble as I may, I need to continue developing my faith from one discovery to another on the way to satisfaction or fulfillment.

The introduction of free will into the discussion does little to explain why there are so many natural catastrophes, fatal collisions on highways, and diseases like cancer. There is little consolation in saying, "If people were just good, something different would have happened to curb all the sufferings and death in the world," because we would still have natural catastrophes to explain. Furthermore, why do some people suffer more than others, and some are beset with more terrible outcomes than others? Could it be that God did not have anything to do with bringing on these problems in the first place? I think so.

From the perspective of what has just been discussed, I realized I could not stop with my discovery about the qualities of God. I had to continue my journey of faith, carrying in my bag of beliefs a new expectation that I would eventually arrive at answers to the obvious contradictions set before me. Contradictions and doubts reside not only in the initial definitions received in my youth but even more so in complex definitions as my faith matures. The important quality of my faith is that there will not be a total satisfaction in any discovery about God.

As a youth, the discovery element in my faith was minimal. I had, at all times, the defining terms set before me by educators. I realize now that my developing faith was always seeking input from others. I needed to fill the empty spaces with a sense of certainty that others before me had provided. My parents and teachers would tell me, "That is the way it is. Do not question it, and no arguing about it because you would just be arguing with God."

A breakthrough with regard to the conundrum of good and evil in the world came when I realized that God is not an intervener in the world the way we traditionally perceive Him to be (chapter 4). My background in the evolutionary principles of biology became an important component. My notions of all-powerful and all good cannot apply to how God *should* operate in the world as I see it. Like nature, *God just is*, and we live with His presence in the same way that nature is and we live with it.

Just because a person's evil and immoral conduct devastates my sense of good and could cause harm to an ethical system does not mean that God lacks power, knowledge, and goodness. My understanding of a gentle and nurturing world must include natural calamities when they do occur. My discovery is that the ever-present God just is, and we must live with the whole package of events that happen in our lives. It is not a case of God's ways not being our ways, but rather that nature and humankind do not always see eye to eye on horrible events that happen. To fix this insight in my mind, I conjured up the following message from God: "The Lord said to the inquiring mind, I give, and I take. It is my nature to select the gift of life." Being an evolutionary biologist and a Catholic, the principles of natural selection are always taking on more meaning for me as I live my faith.

Reality versus the Eucharistic Presence

Another discovery for me is the Christian (Catholic) belief that at Mass the Holy Eucharist of bread and wine is transformed into the actual body and blood of Christ. My faith in this doctrinal statement hinged on taking someone's word for it. As a youth, I would kneel in prayerful adoration of Jesus inside a gold-plated monstrance, sitting on the altar or displayed in a procession around the church at special times of the year.

Being incapable of understanding the theology behind transubstantiation at the time, I wholeheartedly accepted that what I was eating and drinking was indeed the body and blood of Christ, our Savior. I had this feeling that, like my family and friends, it was the right thing to believe. Mind you, I felt good engaging in this because it was comforting to know that someone very important was present and within me. I had, at this time, no way of knowing that what I believed in faith was not the same as the reality. I believed the host to be Jesus, not even questioning the facts of the matter. The whole process of believing in Jesus in the Eucharist was indeed an initial definition (from an authority), and at the time, that was good enough for me.

While in the ministry and as a celebrant in the community, I found that I needed to take another journey because this definition of God being in the Eucharist did not satisfy my continued search for God in my life of science. Being educated in science, I found the doctrine of transubstantiation unbelievable and unnecessary. In the real world, one does not say something is physically present without validating that assumption. I know faith is not reality, even though I believe my faith to be important to me. Inspired by modern theological thought (both Catholic and non-Catholic), my search led to a new discovery and insight. The consecrated bread was still bread, and the wine was still wine. Since I *expected* some sort of answer, I began to see the Eucharistic celebration in a new way, a much more intellectually satisfying way.

Not long ago, while visiting friends out of country and attending Mass at their parish, I listened to a priest explain how the bread was transformed into the body of Christ, but when taken in and swallowed, it was no longer the body of Christ. During his homily, he concentrated on explaining why Catholics are really not practicing a form of cannibalism (a major criticism by non-Catholics). Had he stayed on the spiritual level, it would not have been as confusing. However, he meticulously went into detail about how the substance of the body of Christ, physically present, disappeared when the bread disintegrated in the mouth. That was it. The physical Jesus was the physical bread. After my short vacation, I decided to respond in letter form to the priest. Part of my response was as follows:

(On spiritual cannibalism). The issue is about the nature of "substance," (what makes something to be that thing), which is a philosophical construct of the mind from Aristotelian times. It is not directly related to reality (maybe analogically), because "substance" in bread is not verifiable as being anything else physically than the DNA of some kind of unleavened wheat. The same can be said of wine, and the DNA from some kind of grape. Transubstantiation is only a spiritual conjecture, which cannot be physically evidenced at all. The host as Jesus is not physically Jesus, and not a physical reality.

Catholics may think they are consuming the body of Christ, but certainly are not actually cannibals when receiving communion at Mass. At best, Catholics and some other denominations could be considered spiritual cannibals. Lastly, my statement does not mean Christ is not present for and to us, as in the liturgy of the Word and Eucharist. When we bless, break, and share bread, we are in communion with one another as the body of Christ living today. We become the body of Christ when we receive both the "Word" and the breaking of the bread.[24]

My response to the priest was an expression of my discovery. However, I did not receive a response back from the pastor. Apparently, it was not a discovery for him. After a journey around the world of transubstantiation (i.e., the substance of bread becomes the substance of Christ), I arrived knowingly at the same point but saw it in another, more meaningful way. Many years ago, Father John McKenzie, SJ, said it very well in his *Dictionary of the Bible*. When defining a sign for theological students, he said, "For example, the Eucharist is an effective sign for Christian unity, made so by the church being the body of Christ."[25] Father McKenzie was saying that, although a sign is a representation used to indicate something, my discovery is that he meant the bread represented the body of Christ, which, when consumed, becomes the body of Christ for the world.

Many people have not realized or discovered this new insight about Christians being in communion with one another and becoming Christ for others. Father McKenzie may not have totally understood the implication of these words, but *effective sign* is neither the effective reality (other than being a sign) nor a physical reality of any kind other than the material that made up the sign. Another way of looking at the body of Christ could be this: the church (people, not a building) is the body of Christ. The bread (set apart as in a ceremony) is a sign that we are in communion with one another. Receiving the bread tells us that we are invited to be in union with not only Christ but one another as well. Sharing the bread with one another, we become the body of Christ for others.

Discovery of these qualities of God and of the Eucharist were important discoveries for me, not because I arrived at new insights but for what followed from those insights. For me, this was another discovery and quest.

Before I usher you into the last example of discovery leading to a quest, it is important to grasp that there is much more to a discovery experience than just insight into some previously defined theological thought. For me, every discovery generates the need for another journey. The journey is preceded by an expectation that I am going to mature further in my faith experience. In fact, expecting that there is much more about my faith is essential for igniting a deeper faith in God. Is it possible that at some time, there will only be an expectation? I am not sure, but I believe that is what makes a quest interesting.

Survival of the Soul

The final example of my discovery is the most difficult to treat and even to this day leaves some emptiness within me, as well as some questions and doubts in my mind. If only the concept of soul could be accepted as a concept filled with an analogical content. However, that is not the case. The belief that our souls are separate and spiritually distinct entities within our bodies is now a doctrine firmly set in history. It has its origin in several ancient traditions. The Greek tradition given to us from Plato and Aristotle played a dominant role in the traditional dualistic understanding of human nature that we as Christians have inherited and share today. It is very difficult for any religion to consider this unique dualistic existence in any other way, since the body-soul duality is deeply rooted in historical belief and in most cases is considered an unquestionable, nondebatable, as-is reality. What should be seen as an analogy or way of thinking is thought to be the reality of our existence, with no more questions or debate about it. This is an unfortunate circumstance.

As Catholics, we learned from our childhood days that, at conception, God infuses a fertilized egg with the complete human nature of body and soul. The body is a material entity, and the soul an immaterial and immortal entity.[26] For many centuries now, the Christian Church has defined human nature as a unity with two parts, one spiritual (the soul) and one physical (the body). In my early years, I did not question this dictate and doctrine.

It was not until about thirty years ago that I began to question how the soul could fit in with what science has learned about human nature. Personality is about as close as we can get to witnessing and understanding the concept of soul, yet personalities are often totally changed by severe brain trauma and drug abuse. Neuroscientists and psychologists add a great deal of knowledge about how such transformations take place. I believe, little by little, science is whittling away at the traditional belief of the soul being created by God at the time of the union of an egg with a sperm.

The point I am making with the example of the body/soul conundrum is that I have added another insight to my personal discovery about God. I have discovered that Christians need to revisit the treasured belief that God needs to intervene physically in our lives at crucial points. The creation of a soul when each human egg is fertilized appears to be an unproductive way of addressing the idea of a soul.

From the time of the fertilization of an egg to the birth of a child, there has to be allowance for what the principles of evolution bring to the table regarding the origin of humankind. My discovery, at this point, is the insight that God is always present to me in my life, but informing a soul into a cell is not part of that insight. I discovered that God is indeed present to me, but not as an intervener into the arrival of humankind, nor a deity who puts a stamp on a creative act. With regard to a layperson's understanding of the advent of humankind, there must be, in today's world, the inclusion of an evolutionary component. Presently, we possess in common with many primates over 95% percent of our DNA. If we were to go back two million years, the tally would be closer to 100 percent of our DNA shared with hominids who no longer exist except in fossil form. To maintain the belief that what makes Homo sapiens human is the "informing with a soul at the time of fertilization" is a highly questionable belief.

The question now is, how do I look for God when I look for Him in nature? How do I look for God in my own personal life and existence? Expecting that there is something different about how I understand God in my heart does not imply that I am losing my faith in the divine presence. Expectation convinces me that I need to take another journey and, arriving at the word *soul*, see it in a different perspective. My idea of soul is now different from what tradition has taught me. But traditional beliefs are indeed very important for me, at least as a starting point for experiencing God in my life. Roy T. Bennett summed it up very well when he said, "The past is a place of reference, not a place of residence ... a place of learning, not a place of living."[27] Expectation after a spiritual discovery is a living drive to learn more about my past heritage of faith but not necessarily to live in that heritage.

What did I learn about the existence of a soul that is different from what tradition has taught? Since God is not an intervener in what He has created, the concept of the body and soul being distinct entities falls short. It is a way of thinking about how God creates. The concept of soul is an analogy, a construct of the mind, which satisfied the ancient fathers of the church at the time. We need a new analogy at this point. Instead of possessing two entities, one mortal and the other immortal, the individual is one entity, and it is only because we have a need to talk about God's presence here that we hold dear the idea of soul as a spiritual entity. The idea of being immaterial and immortal flows from our minds, born out of the capacity of the mind and its need to express how important God is in the world. Deep down, we need to talk about this experience of God being present in us. For me personally, this is a potent discovery, and the search goes on.

Many scientists maintain something quasi-immaterial about the function of the brain, and we will get to some sort of satisfaction on the matter someday, maybe. What has been important for me is to admit that out of the evolutionary development of the brain comes my need to envision some sort of immateriality to my life. It is not important to maintain a duality of soul and body when, out of the capacity of the mind, a new insight into soul and immortality is discovered. We are very much like a human dynamo,[28] which generates with its mind an infinite capacity. This is what makes us immortal. I can now say I have learned something new about my creator.

In conclusion, the discoveries I have made in my life are insights needing to be questioned. This is what I call my quest, and it requires a constant intellectual movement forward. The realization for me is that new discoveries need to enter into my faith experience. I will always expect to discover insights that need more clarification. If my mind is open to maturing to its full capability, it should always question and be open to expecting a discovery. This is what we are all about in matters of faith. As intellectual beings, we are seeking answers to the world in which we live and answers from our continual search for God. We should never deny or abandon the reality and facts of today in favor of something fabricated for us long ago. Our lives are like unfinished business, with the search and expectation process never ending.

In the following chapter, I will explain what might be endpoints (goals) of a mind never satisfied with unanswered questions and dilemmas.

10

Are There Other Ways of Understanding Eternity? Probably.

As a child, I attended Catholic grade school, where I was taught by very caring and holy nuns who showed an interest in my physical well-being as well as my need to know about God and eternity. I specifically remember a class where the teacher helped us understand what eternity is like. She explained eternity using a timeline that we could understand. She compared eternity to a bird flying around the Empire State Building in New York once a month. As the robin flew around the building, it brushed its wing against the side of the structure. When the building collapsed due to the wing's contact, eternity will have just begun. That story stuck in my mind, and I remember the children in the class were awestruck. I could not begin to imagine how many bird wings it would take just to begin eternity. Eternity was a fearsome idea, especially since we were taught that we would be stuck in one place forever. If that place were hell, it would be terrifying, to say the least.

In this extended chapter, I will treat a variety of subjects in a way that could be upsetting. I ask for your patience as I move through different topics on the traditional ways we view eternity. I will share some insights as to what the early Israelites and early

Christians thought of eternity. Secondly, we will discuss why devotions based on questionable beliefs about the afterlife and eternity should be reexamined. I say this because we should know that sacred images, although important, are temporal and change overtime. We also look at how a quest for God is like an eternal journey. Lastly, I share with you what I think Jesus taught about eternity.

Simply put, my proposal is much like an invitation to think about these matters a little differently. Because there may also be questions in your minds about how we presently understand eternity, I would like to offer some insights into beliefs that could replace ideas we have about what lies ahead after we die.

While waiting for the kingdom of God to be realized, we seem to be looking for a *place where* in the next life, rather than viewing eternity as an experience in this life. We envision a glorified condition rather than a quality that is part of self-fulfillment. When looking at eternity as a location, we can find some comfort in that it offers a sense of confidence and expectation. Being in space and time, it makes sense to expect quasi-material places ahead when we breathe our last. I suggest that we need to reexamine the need for a glorified place to spend eternity.

In His public life, Jesus used metaphors and analogies in abundance, as when He said, "There are many rooms in my Father's house."[29] He did this to counter the greedy expectations of some of his disciples. Jesus used the metaphor about His Father's house to tell His disciples that the kingdom is all-inclusive, and everyone is invited. But I believe another more authentic depiction of the kingdom of God was expressed by Jesus when He said, "The kingdom of God is within you" (Luke 17:21, The Good News Translation).

God the Almighty does not reside as a glorified body somewhere on a paradise-like planet in space. God is not an entity that takes a shape of some kind but is rather a force (presence) that we experience within us. I sincerely believe that when Jesus talked about the kingdom of His Father, He was talking about eternity residing within our believing hearts.

Precisely how and why Jesus made some unusual statements about His Father's kingdom, we will never know for sure. I believe He was hinting at the need to find an eternal value to the good news from the Father, the good news that resides in our hearts, not in some ethereal place out there or up above us among the stars and galaxies. There were many Christian communities spread across the Middle East, and undoubtedly, there were many different understandings of what the kingdom of God meant in various places. However, the belief that there is an eternal nature to God's kingdom (whatever that might be) was universally accepted.

God and Eternity for the Israelites and Early Christians

The early Israelites correctly believed that God has no form. While wandering in the Moab Desert, the leaders of the Hebrew clan commanded their followers not to attempt to create any molten image before which homage was given. During the wars in Leviticus and Judges, the Ark of the Covenant was carried along as a sign of security and victory.[30] The ark was described as something holy but not an object of worship; it was rather a visual sign that a covenant with the one God was in place and was binding forever.

At first, there was probably nothing inside the ark, except for a felt sense of power or wonder. Legend has it that Moses's tablets of the commandments were placed inside a gold-lined box that could have been the ark. Later rabbinical tradition has a vessel of manna and the rod of Aaron. What is important is that when the ark was present, the Israelites usually won their battles. When the ark was absent, battles were often lost. McKenzie described the meaning and importance of the Ark of the Covenant very well when he said:

> Thus the Ark was the symbol of Yahweh's [Lord God] personal presence, the place where atonement was received, where divine communications were granted. The Ark was carried into battle to symbolize Yahweh's kingship and leadership. It was also the symbol of the covenant of Yahweh with Israel: He was present because He had elected them as His people and imposed upon them the commandments which the Ark contained.[31]

The ark was holy and important because the Israelites received divine guidance from it. At the same time, the leaders delivered oracles from its location. When the ark was present, the all-powerful God was on their side. Unlike many ancient civilizations in Egypt and Mesopotamia, the Israelites generally had no image or carving of a God. However, in a moment of weakness, many of Moses's followers felt they needed to carve golden images of calves. The point is that humankind has a desperate need to quantify, or at least set aside, a place dedicated to the holiness of God, and His power had to be quantified in some way for purposes of acquiring spiritual direction. The Israelites needed God on their side. We entertain the same thoughts about the kingdom of God when we think of heaven as a place where, rather than a quality of life within a believer.

The restoration of the former majesty of Israel was foremost in the mind of the Jews at the time of Christ. The same kind of kingdom was in the mind of Jesus's disciples. Since many prophets in the

Old Testament predicted the restoration of the kingdom of Israel through a Messiah, Jesus had a hard time convincing them otherwise. In most early books of the Bible, the idea of eternity was applied to God on His throne forever. Although somewhat vague, the eternity concept also applied to God, with humankind praising Him forever. God's blessings were thought to be eternal, with little emphasis on an individual's personal placement in heaven or eternity.

In our Christian tradition, the meaning of the kingdom of God is in eternity, but the kingdom is also a place *where*. In eternity, there is no *where*, no time, and the kingdom of God is an experience that has no boundaries. The Ark of the Covenant was not an eternal experience but at best an instructional experience for the Israelites. However, the basis of a new relationship with God for all Christians is a new covenant, which involves a belief in heaven being both eternal and somewhere containing glorified bodies. If we are to move ahead in our understanding of the kingdom of God being from within, then this concept of eternity being somewhere needs to be reexamined.

I suggest a new look at the kingdom of God as being a continual discovery of something that is always a bit beyond our grasp. For me, the discovery that the kingdom of God and eternity could be tied to a drive for self-fulfillment is exciting, because it is a drive that never ends. Is it possible that eternity is a never-ending movement of belief? I believe so.

An Experience of the Eternal Involves an Unfulfilled Quest for God

Given the insights Jesus proposed about the kingdom of God being in our hearts and not somewhere else, my intent now is to explain what the implications might be. To say that the kingdom of God is here and not somewhere else does not negate the traditional idea of eternity, but it will be a different kind of insight. This insight expresses itself as a discovery and a quest for fulfillment, not something pursued as an afterlife experience. If the kingdom of God is not *out there* or *some place* to be experienced, then the idea of what it means to be eternal must necessarily be altered, or at least viewed from a different perspective. This new discovery of eternity is my continual quest for a more fulfilling experience of God. The experience of God is not a total fulfilling experience for me in my life, and probably not in a life hereafter either. My continued quest for a God becomes a discovery of a new kind of eternity, with the kingdom of God residing in my heart.

There is another thought that presents itself in my discussion on eternity. It has to do with issues and contradictions within the traditional idea of eternity (hinted at in chapter 4). If you remember, the proposals in chapter 4 required a new paradigm. If I take the idea of eternity out of the space-time continuum, then there is no room for an intervention by God in my life. The reason I say this is that God is the ground of my being. If there is an eternal presence to God, then there is no need to entertain an idea that God ought to recreate on our behalf an event in our space-time existence. I speak of God my creator, but He is not such by way of a distinct creative act in time. He is fully eternally present. When there is no beginning and no ending to God's creation, then God's creative activity is happening now. You and I are an ongoing creative act of God. You have noted that the creation wheel gets larger in time. It is because creation is ongoing in our lives. With a new idea of creation, we now have an opportunity to look at eternity in a different way.

The eternal deity is always present in the same way to all humans, regardless of where humanity is in its evolutionary development.

The eternal is in everything and everywhere, with everything and everywhere being grounded in the eternal. This is not the same as pantheism—that is, God being everywhere, and everything is God. To say that God (His presence) is in everything is not to say that God *is* everything, and everything *is* God.

If this new paradigm from chapter 4 is reasonable, the following controversial issues need to be addressed:

1. There is nothing transcendent or immanent about an eternal entity, because the eternal is the very ground of our being (always present).
2. God is eternal but not in our way of thinking in space and time.
3. God does not intervene to make something right or to protect someone from harm.
4. God is not on our side, as opposed to someone else's side.
5. God does not adjust His creative act to solve a given emergency or problem at a time in evolutionary history.
6. God cannot be manipulated in any way.
7. Our bodies will not be resurrected after death, at least not in the traditional sense.
8. There is no glorified place where we are able to enjoy an existence as resurrected individuals.
9. The kingdom of God is here and now, as God is eternally present to us.
10. The kingdom of God in our hearts is our eternity.

The above statements are controversial. I chose to present them now, rather than place them in chapter 4 with the creation wheel paradigm. It is my hope that the intervening chapters have prepared you for these statements. The above controversial issues do not destroy our faith in the eternal but rather focus on the importance of finding the eternal presence now. What lies ahead for us after death cannot be known in space-time and will never be known here in this life. After death, an ascent to a new life is in the realm of a belief given to us by religious educators.

The point I am making is that we should not look at what is ahead of us but look at what is in the present. We can never know with certainty what lies ahead using the traditional idea of eternity. We simply do not know what eternity might be, because eternity is unknowable, and the present as opposed to eternity will always be bridged with an act of faith.

I would like to spend a bit more time on our quest for the eternal and how it relates to our need to be happy. I came across a quote on happiness by Margaret Lee Runbeck, who said, "Happiness is not a station [state] to arrive at, but a manner of traveling."[32] I believe that she meant our personal self-fulfillment is not a destination to be reached but a journey to be made. Such an idea carries a good deal of weight in my opinion. Self-fulfillment (I would like to call it happiness) is not a static thing at all. It is an ongoing experience yet to be finished, and it will never be a complete experience. This is what I call a spiritual quest.

As discussed in my chapter on happiness (chapter 2), most people erroneously see happiness as an experience based on material accomplishments and an amount of public acceptance. We are caught up in the idea that accomplishments (finished items in life) are the measuring sticks of happiness. However, happiness is in the mind and not in accomplishments that are static items in our lives. Accomplishments are somewhat outside ourselves and beyond us, cloaked in some outside recognition.

A Continual Quest for God Fuels Happiness

Far from being a property or characteristic that we own, happiness always involves a continual invitation, a call to be someone better. I am not completely satisfied with the way I am. I am a cup, which is never full. It is true that we can experience a degree of satisfaction with what we have *accomplished*, but that is not *self-fulfillment* or happiness.

When we talk about the search for God in our lives being a never-ending journey in life, it is similar to a never-ending experience of happiness. If spiritual happiness is the journey itself, then our search for God is an expectation that is never quite complete. It does not mean that expecting to learn more about God will leave us unhappy. Happiness is like an unending journey of expectation. If we think that on any given day we have found God, and we are satisfied with the personal experience of happiness, this understanding is not of God but rather from what someone has told us about God.

In her statement on happiness, Runbeck does not imply that when you have acquired some measure of wealth, you will continually need to satisfy the urge and seek after more things and greater wealth. I believe, on the contrary, that she is saying happiness is not a quantifiable thing at all but rather a special mindset acquired on a journey. In other words, your journey is what provides the framework for happiness. You are expected to fill that framework with fulfilling experiences that generate the kind of satisfaction we call happiness. It is not things (material items, etc.) but only the immeasurable items we call experiences.

Furthermore, Runbeck's implications do not stop at this point. The consequence is that people find themselves incomplete yet continue seeking and enjoying more deeply these new experiences. These experiences in themselves have no finality, no ending. In my mind, this is what I call heaven or a heavenly experience. I call this experience a God experience, and it can be our experience of eternity now.

Following my belief that heaven is not a place where, we can now look at eternity as the journey itself, which is in this life and not somewhere else after we die. It is true, we live in a material world, but what we can produce is oftentimes immaterial, even though our thoughts are stored in electrochemical packets in our brains. The phenomenon of love would be a good example. Well-being can be measured (i.e., pulse, blood pressure, kidney and brain function, along with many other functions of the body), but happiness, like love, is much more than serotonin, dopamine, or other specifically stimulating chemicals produced by the body. Being at peace is an amazing experience in our lives, almost as if it is an experience of divine presence. Few people today can extricate themselves from the material realm. If people desire the acceptance of others and need to exercise power over others to the point that these accomplishments are paramount, they miss the idea of what brings peace and purpose in their lives.

Why We Need to Continue the Quest for God

I hope this discussion has not given the impression that I am disparaging anyone's particular stance on matters of eternity. If you find satisfaction in the traditional ideas of the kingdom of God, eternity, and spiritual happiness, that is fine. Go with it. My point is that such views do not satisfy me.

The quest for God has now become an unfulfilled expectation. I believe this is what eternity is for me, and I find this to be acceptable. Also, I continually insist on the need to look for fulfillment in God through the kingdom of which Jesus spoke. You may ask, what is that kingdom of God on earth? It is the human embodiment of the good news that Jesus brings from the Father. What should matter to us as believers is not what happens after death but how we live our lives as the embodiment of God's Word worked out now, in our present lives. The human embodiment of the good news of Jesus Christ can now be eternalized. The challenge for the traditional Christian is to let go of the idea that the eternal kingdom of God is found after death, rather than being the eternal presence of God here in us now.

Eternity Is Not an Endpoint but a Journey

I believe in the future that we will not understand eternity in the same way as tradition has taught. There is a way of illustrating how eternity will be more like a journey than the endpoint of a relationship with God. Eternity can be part of the present, just as the kingdom of God has arrived and resides in the hearts of Christian believers in the present. It is not my intent to deny any traditional idea of eternity offered but to suggest that the kingdom of God is not *out there* somewhere, to be experienced at the end of a journey. Rather, the journey is the kingdom now, part of the quest for fulfillment, and that will always be a part of eternity now.

At the beginning of this discussion, I stressed that at no time do I imply that a novel idea of eternity requires the dismissal of any images, practices, devotion, and experiences that continue to enrich our lives. In the past, rituals and ceremonies formed a strong foundation for keeping a Christian community together, and new types of such devotions will form the framework for Christians in the future. What enriches our lives should be treasured as a way of strengthening our spirit as we continue our journey toward fulfillment.

Now I would like to share with you some traditional stories and images that will probably *not* accompany us on our journey into the future, and will not be part of our experience of eternity. After discussing the common understanding of the Adam and Eve story, I will discuss the devotion to the Sacred Heart of Jesus and the Immaculate Heart of Mary. These stories and images have been emblazoned into our Catholic minds for decades. The Sacred Heart devotion is at least nine hundred years old and grew out of a pious devotion to Jesus. This devotion thrived because people believed that men and women sinned and needed the redemptive suffering of Jesus. Humankind needed to be saved. This is why, in church circles, the Adam and Eve myth was of extreme importance.

Somehow, the suffering Jesus, pictured with the crown of thorns around His heart, calls out to all believers the need to bathe in a devotion to the suffering servant whose heart was pierced out of love for us. At present, science brings to the table some important discoveries that will change the framework of devotions arising from thinking that our sinful nature resulted from a supposed original fall of humankind.

The Adam and Eve Myth

Nearly all devotions occurring over the centuries were promulgated because of a deep conviction that we arrive on earth in a sinful state and therefore need to be saved. However, science tells us that we arrived on this planet not from any divine intervention, which infuses a specially created soul into a human body, but from the creative act of God called biological evolution. Although we are special, we are simply the product of an evolutionary process over several million years, and our origins are polygenetic. By this I mean there were many hominid groups and species, which eventually led to Homo sapiens. The discovery of a need for a deity came much later in this evolutionary process, well after the movement out of Africa (around one million BCE) and probably just before civilizations began to be formed (50,000–100,000 BCE).

The story of a fall of our first parents arose out of Mesopotamian beliefs, which were largely myths with morals attached. The original sin doctrine arose after the birth of the Christian religion and probably from the teachings of St. Paul. This fabrication was not preached by Christ but arose out of the church's need to have a reason why Christ had to suffer and die such a horrible death. However, there were no *first parents* in history, and there was no such thing as a historical original sin (eating of the forbidden fruit). So, we ask, why is it necessary to say anyone had to die to rid us of our innate sinful nature? For a partial answer, let us look at devotions connected at least indirectly to our supposed fall from grace.

The Suffering Sacred Heart and the Immaculate Heart

The origins of devotion to the Sacred Heart of Jesus appear initially as early as the eleventh century when pious Christians meditated on the five wounds of Jesus. Later on, devotion specifically to the Sacred Heart arose in the seventeenth century and again in the nineteenth century. The overall intent was to expose the suffering servant (Jesus, Son of God) as also human and to show that through His suffering, He has redeemed the world. There are many trappings to this devotion, but Jesus always appears with a pierced heart, which is supposed to give comfort to the devout Christian.

What is interesting is that the images (paintings and pictures) always portray Jesus as an individual with physical features of the contemporary male face of the time. Each century has tales of miraculous apparitions with the elaborate trappings of an attractive king or prince of the time. In modern times, the imagery retains a royal garb but displays a modern, contemporary Western Caucasian appearance. My point here is to show how, from an ancient belief relating to our origins, a devotion surfaced that distracts us from the reason why Jesus preached in Palestine in the first place. Jesus came to share the good news of the Father. That was it. Jesus died in the process, and He needs us to continue His work.

Devotion to the heart of Mary arose out of a belief that the only person who could give birth to the Son of God had to be born pure, free from the evil spectra of the fall of Adam and Eve and the plague of original sin. The womb that gave birth to the Son of God must necessarily be virginal and sinless from the moment of conception. Devotion to Mary centered upon her differences from the rest of humankind, and we look up to her as a mediatrix or intercessor between Jesus and God the Father. Devotion to the pure heart of Mary actually refers to the interior life of Mary, including her joys and sorrows, as well as the love she has for Jesus, our Savior. These qualities are probably what purified her.

During the Middle Ages, there were many devotions to Mary. In the fifteenth century, we have specific allusions to the heart of Mary. It was at the end of the nineteenth century that reference to the pure heart of Mary became widespread. In the early twentieth century, the use of *immaculate* showed up in this specific devotion to Mary. Remarkable similarities between the heart of Mary and the heart of Jesus arose in graphic images of a pierced heart with girding thorns, and these images always portrayed modern

Western Caucasian facial characteristics. In eternity, which glorified presence of the Sacred Heart and Immaculate Heart will we be witnessing? Will it be our contemporary fabrications or the presence of a first-century Middle Eastern glorified body? I speak with a bit of irony here, knowing that pictures of Jesus and Mary are specifically rendered to easily elicit devotion from a believer at a given time in history.

Most Christians know that the paintings of both Jesus and Mary express the imagery of the time: Spanish, French, and other cultures, the majority of which include the facial presentation of the Teutonic race along with its trappings. The same error occurs to this day. Not one of the graphic illustrations mirrors the characteristic of the Middle Eastern race, which was that of Jesus and Mary, but rather depicts an acceptable person of the Western culture. These are interesting observations but relatively unimportant overall.

Devotion to many of the saints follow the same pattern as do the Jesus and Mary devotions, but I have shared enough to help you see how such types of devotional images are presently used to enhance our faith response. Possibly, we will be creating our own sacred images in the years to come. Please be aware that I am not dismissing such types of devotion as irrelevant and lacking faith-enhancing powers for the contemporary believer. What I am saying is that such types of devotion will become less and less helpful for supporting our faith journey in the future. In the following chapter, I will treat the value of images, in as much as they support our prayer life. However, it would be best first to look at what we have received as Jesus's words about eternity in order to enhance our journey toward fulfillment.

What Did Jesus Say about Eternity?

It is interesting to discuss what happens after we die. But what really matters is how we live the kingdom of God on earth. What happens after death is a matter of personal belief and conjecture. Real expectation and quest for God is not in the hereafter but in the present. Jesus did speak about the last judgment day and the many places in His Father's kingdom for His followers. However, He always preached in parable, metaphor, and allegory forms. We have no idea how Jesus's thought on the matter may have been altered, especially after the early Christian communities realized the kingdom was not coming soon, and not even in the foreseeable future.

I believe that Jesus's words on heaven and the afterlife arose from the kingdom of God being within us. Unfortunately, the original Jewish quest for the restoration of the kingdom of Israel was strong and ultimately became, for the early Christians, a quest for an eternal and external kingdom, with heaven being up there rather than existing in our hearts. Non-Jewish converts to Christianity probably had some questions about restoring the kingdom of Israel. The new converts from Greece, Syria, and other countries within the Roman Empire held little attachment to the new kingdom of Israel that Jesus's disciples thought the promised Messiah was to restore. The Roman Empire was troublesome enough, let alone another kingdom to serve and to which taxes had to be paid.

A quest for fulfillment should be the answer to the believer's idea of eternity. All else is really a fabrication that changes with the times, just as our beliefs about the matter of eternity evolve. Jesus really did say, "The kingdom of God is within you" and "Unless you are born again in water and spirit you cannot enter the kingdom of God."³³ Is there possibly something else Jesus meant, if He was not speaking about being born again in another resurrected corporeal form? I think so, as I explain below.

Because they did not understand Jesus, the disciples ridiculed Him for presenting this strange idea of the kingdom of heaven. The disciples were educated within the traditional idea that the kingdom of God automatically meant the restoration of the kingdom of Israel. They even fought over who was going to sit in what place in the new kingdom. However, Jesus meant that by being born again through the ritual of baptism, we are now in possession of the kingdom of God. Jesus is implying that the good news of His Father (the Word of God) requires a human body for expression. To make the good news effective, there is a need to be born into the Holy Spirit with the waters of baptism.

What happened in the centuries after Christ's death was the formation of the institutional church, which became synonymous with the kingdom of God on earth. This development was an unfortunate circumstance. But what else could the Christians do at the time? Jesus did not come back, and there was no last judgment and end of the world. The coming of the Holy Spirit, as exemplified many times in the Acts of the Apostles, now became the force holding the early community together for survival.

Soon after the events in the Acts of the Apostles, Jesus's expected kingdom became the institutional church by default. Within a century, the institutional church fell victim to all the imperfections of any ordinary organization or societal structure throughout history. Greed, lust for power, and domination began to appear, just as they do in all societies in history. The institution had to persist, and so the church fell into a self-serving mode to ensure its own existence. It became the official teaching authority of

Christ. I am convinced the institutional church, not long after its formation, became synonymous with eternal kingdom of God on earth, instead of the divine presence (the kingdom of God) being within the believer.

I understand that many traditional beliefs are being challenged at this point, but if we are to move ahead with a credible Christian perspective for the future, it is my belief that a major concession must take place. We can continue to relish a belief about eternity being a place where, and fulfillment being in a place with God after we die. However, I believe that such a view of the quest for religious fulfillment, with resurrected bodies rejoined with an immortal soul, will not stand the test of time. Relevance and credibility are crucial for educated people today.

The analogies and metaphors in parable form used by Jesus were his way of teaching the good news of His Father. The disciples and early Christians took these stories as reality. I believe the never-ending quest for fulfillment is truly the only experience of eternity we can have at this time. We are invited to put our efforts into working out what this means for us. We can continue to nurture our belief that eternity is separate from the kingdom of God in our hearts, but I see it as a belief that will always end up as unexplainable and will lead us nowhere.

In conclusion, I am not dismissing traditional belief in the hereafter. What I am proposing is that our ideas about the hereafter are less important than experiencing what eternity could mean for us in this life. What happens after we die is unknowable. It is only by our faith and hope that we pray for a continued form of existence after death. I am proposing that it is time to look at the possibility that there is no eternity as it is defined by our Christian tradition.

These traditional ideas about the hereafter are not as important as finding out and experiencing eternity in our lives now. We will always carry within us traditional thoughts solidly implanted into our hearts since our childhood days. However, if the kingdom of God is, as Jesus preached it to be, in our hearts, it will have to be more than just a message about eternity somewhere. Just as Jesus can only make His message known through us, so also, as Christians, we need to admit that the kingdom of God will be an eternity experienced in our lives now.

11

Are We Creating Our Ideas about God? So What?

In earlier chapters, I talked about the qualities of God (all-powerful, all knowing, and all benevolent). These qualities are descriptions of what we think a perfect being should be like. Although we cannot possibly know what God is, we still think of Him as always perfect and unchanging. Because our nature is to be imperfect, in need of change, we automatically think of God as someone who has no need to change—that is, who is *finished* or *completed*.

However, we, as humans, know we have to change in order to survive. Sir Winston Churchill put it very well when he said, "To improve is to change, to be perfect is to change often."[34] But when we think of God as perfect, we think of Him as never changing. However, our *ideas* of Him change. Could it be that our ideas about God change because we are always changing? Although God may never change, we are constantly creating new perceptions of Him in order to make Him relevant to our times. And when we alter our ideas about God, we experience His divine presence somewhat differently. I believe all of these changing ideas about God and how He is present to us can be very beneficial.

In this chapter, I would like to look more closely at how our ideas of God have changed over the centuries. Christian tradition has certainly played a major role in how we look at God. Just as a child's perception of God changes, from a stern figure who blows sailors across turbulent waters to a more inviting figure, so also our adult ideas of God will change. We are constantly discovering a new understanding of God and what He wants us to do as we move along in our spiritual lives. Is it possible that learning more about God has something to do with our learning more about what it means to be human? I believe so.

Are God's Ways Our Ways? Probably Not

Culture probably plays an important role as we constantly reshape how we understand God and how we communicate our beliefs. The sacred icons of God in the third and fourth centuries are not the same as those of the painted images and sculptures of the fourteenth and fifteenth centuries. Similarly, important figures in the New Testament as we visualize them today are different from those in the past. I believe that we are creating not only different images of God but perceptions of His will and intent for us as well. Is this good for the modern believer, or is this an unfortunate circumstance? It is an interesting topic for sure. I would like to illustrate how we create our ideas about God with a contemporary event that happened in my own city of Calgary in Canada.

With the onset of COVID-19, a corona virus that plagued the entire world, restrictions were set in place to curb the spread in local areas. Governments curtailed travel in and out of countries. Local businesses were shut down, and services were limited to prevent the spread of this contagious virus. In my hometown of Calgary, gatherings were limited to a fraction of the overall capacity of the venues, whether they were in churches, convention centers, or outdoor spaces.

The city fined a local Baptist church after it was warned several times for being in breach of the limitations and health rules set in place during the pandemic. The pastor said in response to the penalty, "I understand many will not agree, but our gatherings are essential. They are essential because we are declaring the truth of Jesus Christ, and how one can be forgiven and reconciled to God and have eternal life ... it is impossible for us to obey God with these temporary restrictions."[35] Somehow, the pastor believed he had a privileged communication with God that said it was okay for the congregation to convene in unlawful numbers without masks.

However, the Bible does not say that believers must convene in large numbers and without masks during religious gatherings. For this pastor, his perception of God was that, regardless of the conditions of the time, He required mandatory attendance, without masks, in order for the people to be forgiven, reconciled to Him, and have eternal life.[36] This pastor in Calgary had a perception of God with which most churches in Calgary took issue. Although we believe this pastor's understanding of God is incorrect, we cannot falsify it, because it is impossible to demonstrate in any way what God is, likes, or wants. Disagreeing with someone does not mean that they are wrong. We cannot prove or disprove their ideas with certainty, even if the injunctions they refer to are not found in the Bible.

Two months later, the same pastor was fined once again for a breach of the COVID restrictions. In response to the additional penalties, the pastor had this to say:

> We are not against all rules and health measures. However, we cannot comply with rules that make what we essentially do as a church impossible ... And to be clear, it is Jesus Christ, not civil government that defines what is essential for the gathered church."[37]

The first and most obvious point here is that the *pasto*r has defined what is essential and what Jesus wants and expects of His believers. Personally, I am at a loss as to how he received this insight into God's will for us. It is also beyond my understanding, how, in a civilized society, an individual or group of individuals could believe it was necessary to put a larger community at risk of sickness and/or death because of a supposed divine revelation that encouraged them to violate health restrictions. Officials who are trying to protect the health and well-being of the citizens put health restrictions in place. The pastor contravened these restrictions by proclaiming that his own ways are God's ways.

The second point is also directly to the purpose of this chapter. Throughout the history of Christianity (and all religions, for that matter), leaders in communities have been defining the nature and qualities of their God. Put in a more simplified context, religious beliefs and ordinances have taken on a unique expression, in accord with the time and place of each belief.

What is ironic is how preachers have twisted basic meanings in the Bible. The book of Genesis has written that we are made in the image of God.[38] What is actually happening is that we are fashioning God in our own image. One of the parishioners of the church cited above was quoted as saying, "We're devastated by what has happened [pastor being incarcerated]. We have the right to go to church and worship God the way that God tells us to."[39]

The Roman Catholic Church is not any better than other churches in this regard, because it falls into the same delusion as this particular Calgary Baptist Church. For example, a proclamation from Rome legislates a moral obligation to attend Mass on Sundays. If deliberately disobeyed, the church says that the sinner commits a mortal sin and, if not confessed, will certainly suffer the fires of hell. I remember a popular actor on a comedy show, responding to this by saying, "I didn't know God was always taking attendance." It is a hilarious response, but unfortunately, such types of church proclamations still occur even to this day. The church has no power to condemn a person to hell for violating a human-made rule. If there is a hell, it is God's prerogative!

Humankind, in a sense, has always been creating its understanding and perception of God. This is nothing new. Whether from indoctrinations, dogmas, encyclicals, or sermons from the pulpit, we have received numerous man-made ideas about the nature and the will of God. These ideas can neither be proved nor disproved. They exist to tell us more about God, what we should believe, and how we should act at a given time in history. The truth is we have been creating God in our own image from the beginning, regardless of what the Bible says.

Creating God's Will for Us

Even if all the things we have learned about God have been creations from the minds of religious leaders, is this situation necessarily always a bad thing? I would have to say no, it is not. In fact, all that we have learned from our youth about God comes from a discovery within the minds of teachers and others in authority. But as adults, all that we know about God comes from more than just what leaders or institutions have told us. What we have learned also comes from a discovery that we pursue in a quest to learn more about God. Our inadequate perceptions and images of God and His will for us will eventually fail, as these ideas will be found unfit for our more contemporary belief. What we believe is God's will for us is what we have defined and think we are obliged to follow. Our perception of God is given to us as a human command to do something, rather than a given idea directly from Him of what He is like and wants us to do.

This creative process does not lessen our faith but can ground it just where it should be—that is, in our minds. As we move ahead with our faith, we assimilate many views. Some beliefs will persist in our collective minds for centuries. Incorrect beliefs will fall by the wayside, eventually giving way to new religious expressions.

Our faith should never stand still but continually evolve as we discover more and more about the divine presence. Past understandings are revelations and discoveries in the historical past. But we do not live in the past; we learn from it. If we live in the past, we will die in the past, with nothing to provide for future generations. If our faith is alive in the present, it is never static. With new definitions and discoveries, we can move forward, looking for a better and more satisfying presence of God in our lives. Indeed, we create our beliefs. To this day, we are creating our perceptions and images of how God is present to us in our lives. I believe that these creative perceptions are part of the way we learn more about our creator.

To explain the above thought in another way, I would like to refer to the earlier discussion with regard to definition, discovery, and quest. Having understood the images of God as defined for me, I now journey in my mind and heart, only to arrive at the same place and see the same words and concepts from a different perspective. I see the same thing (concept), but I see it as new for the first time. This process is, of course, what we call a discovery process, which should leave further questions in our mind. If we are honest, these questions will lead us into another journey for an even more fulfilling perception of what God's presence means for us now. That is the way it should be—a continual journey or quest.

My point is that we are actually creating our images and perceptions of God as we move on in maturing our faith in God. We are creating a deeper understanding with each discovery. This is beneficial because unless we change religiously as we grow in our faith, our understanding of God will fall behind and become a remnant of a defined belief of the past. As we journey with our faith into the future, we change, and the experience of God in our lives becomes something new for us.

In this discussion, it is important to understand that when we are creating our perceptions of God, we are not at any time creating God. We are creating ideas about the divine presence in our lives. I am not saying that God exists only inside our minds; what I am saying is that, as we move along in faith, we develop a further understanding and appreciation for the divine presence in our lives. All of our images and perception of God are within a space-time context. However, God is not limited or confined to our space-time framework. We cannot comprehend or define God or any eternal quality with our physical measuring sticks.

Revelations of the early fathers of the church are revelations from the past for humankind to treasure, but not as if they are the real and only true revelation. They are stepping-stones for us into a future belief and discovery. This does not negate a lasting value to traditional beliefs and practices offered to us. What a revelation tells us is that an idea will always be an unfulfilling concept or value. We should remember that all past revelations about God are limited by the context of the time and were more valuable for people of a past time than for us now. As we learn more about God, we are urged to redefine and rediscover the presence of God. This form of inspiration should give us confidence and assurance that we are moving closer to a fulfilling experience that we can call eternity.

The Need for Sacred Images in Prayer

I want to share one last thought on the notion that we are creating the images and perceptions we have about God, as opposed to experiencing His presence among us. Past beliefs can be a terrific source of solace and comfort for us at any age. We celebrate religious festivals handed down to us because they are extremely important. Communities celebrating together in any form of liturgical act, even if just praying together, can give testimony to the presence of God. Prayer facilitates a new discovery of the kingdom within us. Like pictures on our living room wall, sacred images become etched in our minds, and we recall them each time we experience God in our lives.

Prayer is particularly meaningful when we recall defined images of Jesus, His mother, Mary, and other figures who have gone before us. The use of descriptions for saints, whether they are adjectives or simple descriptions, reminds us of the importance of God's kingdom within us. The kingdom must involve believing people. Just the prayer, "Lord Jesus, Holy Mary, Faithful Joseph, you are my strength," can be very powerful when attached to a defined image in our minds. In prayer, it is not about asking for something. Rather, it is about accepting God's presence as a powerful support for us in good times and bad times.

What is important in prayer is not our mind's image of a holy figure. Images constantly come and go. It is the discovery that a figure has certain qualities that we understand as wonderful. Jesus is indeed lord over our hearts. Mary offers us the kind of love and affection that we always long for in our lives. Joseph exemplifies the kind of devotion we can mirror in our lives, as all of us are called to be faithful manifestations of Christ for others.

Discoveries about God should generate what we call the experience of a divine presence. Images we have of God may define something in our minds, but a continued experience of God's presence should be the goal of any religious inquiry. I believe images provide the knowledge and recognition content, and then discovery generates this new experience, which is the purpose of a good prayer life. Devotion to any important saintly figure can now become part of the kingdom of God in our hearts. The images we constantly refer to can help as part of our personal and community belief. These defined figures, although continually being modified by us, can last a lifetime, as long as the experience of the kingdom of God is alive in our hearts.

This need for images of our own creation is deeply felt by those who experience loss of a loved one, or by a person suffering personal sickness and maladies, leaving him or her at the point of death. We should, at no time, belittle or cast aside items of belief that others treasure, just because a picture, image, or practice may be outdated and out of the context in which it was developed. The presence of God is felt in many ways, and all of us are at different places in our search for God. All of us are on our own journeys, with specific needs for experiencing God in our lives. Be happy that at any point we can say we are on our journey to fulfillment, a journey into the encompassing presence of God. The images and perception of God might be different and even unique, but that does not really matter. We are on our own journey, not someone else's.

In conclusion, we can say, "No, we have not created God and never will create God." However, I believe we have created images and likenesses of God in our minds, and we hold onto them dearly, as if they were the absolute and unchanging view of God. With all due respect to the biblical writers, we are now beginning to realize that God did not create humankind in His own image. Humankind creates images of God in its own likeness within a specific time context. We can say the same about God's will for us. We have created these ideas of what we think God wants us to do. Being restricted in space and time, we can only create images of what we think an infinite God is, what he is about, and what His will might be for us. But this is a fortunate outcome for us, because in a religious community, we can solidify these human-made images and perceptions for others to understand and possibly accept as holy models for good living.

The experience of the divine presence is not entirely of our own intellectual making. The experience of God's presence is what happens when we peel away the skin of an orange to get at the fruit (the divine presence). The skins we peel away are like the created ideas, insights that support our faith, but they are time restrictive and are replaceable in the future by new images and supports. The experience of the divine presence is always within us. It is like the long-lasting taste of a sweet orange. The ideas we have of God are good, but as we mature in our experience of God, these ideas will always take on a new form, though the experience will last a lifetime.

An experience of God's presence is essential and should be with us always. His presence is as real to us as the air we breathe and cannot see. An ancient Buddha directive from the past still stands firm in my mind, "Do not believe in something because I told you; believe it because you experience it yourself." This has been an important directive for me. The experience of God's presence is always more important than any firm idea I have of God.

Lastly, we do not stop with any defined image or perception. If we are true to ourselves, we will never be satisfied with what we have created about God. We are not perfect and have no idea of perfection, only that we must change often in this journey to fulfillment. To be incomplete in a spiritual sense is always a healthy state. But the divine presence of God is always here, with us in good times and in challenging times. As we continue to create our images and perceptions of God, we are being propelled forward from a defined idea into another discovery. The movement forward to fulfillment then becomes a quest, a journey that will never end, and we can call that experience of eternity an experience of God. In the next chapter, we will discuss what an idea of eternity can mean now.

12

Is It Possible to Experience Eternity Now? Why Not?

It has been many years now since I have looked at a *Peanuts* cartoon, but I remember one picture very well, and it has to do at least in part with what I am about to share with you in this chapter. Charlie Brown was sitting on the edge of a dock overlooking a vast, beautiful blue lake. He looked over at Snoopy, his dog, and said, "We only live once, Snoopy." Without taking his eyes off the lake, Snoopy responded, "Wrong, we only die once. We live every day!" The point of Snoopy's response, I am sure, was that we need to be concerned more about living and remembering all the wonderful things that happen in our lives, rather than worrying about the one time when we will pass away. Charlie had a habit of looking pessimistically at all the experiences he had in his young life. As a result, it seemed like misfortunes were always piling up at his door. Snoopy was much more carefree and seemed like he was always happy and enjoying life with his friends. I believe that Snoopy's idea was that we should live life, enjoy life as if it were eternity for us, and not worry about death.

We would do well to remember that the events happening in our lives are just that—events and not life itself. This is not an easy attitude to maintain, but our attitude determines whether we are optimistic or are always hanging up our coats on the crosses that come our way. Perhaps we believe that life has been hard on us, and we just cannot wait until we enter into a better kind of life after death. However, the fact is that living and enjoying each moment is probably the only kind of eternity we can enjoy or comprehend today, although our faith may urge us to think otherwise.

As difficult as it may seem, it is important for Christians to place the eternal nature of the kingdom of God in the present. How do we access this kingdom? We access it through living the good news of Jesus as He preached it and living as if the kingdom of God is in our hearts right now. I believe that thinking I will have that "piece of pie in the sky when I die" offers little solace and will not be the prevailing thought of believers in the future. I am not a prophet, but the idea that God is out there somewhere is not as important as treating everyone as if we were living God's eternal kingdom here and now. God's kingdom here on earth needs to be the important focus for us. We should live and show love in the present and not be yearning for some promised place on the other side of our earthly existence.

We can experience eternity in the here and now. Given the quest for God being unending, there is no other way we can comprehend eternity outside the journey we are on right now. If the faith we have is in the eternal, then what we mean by the eternal must change. It is possible that eternity is not a *forever some place*, as in the traditional understanding of the word *eternal*. It may mean we need to continue our quest for the eternal as the present experience of God in our lives.

The unending quest is what makes us eternal. There is no validated reality of eternity; eternity will always be a matter of faith, the contents of which are largely hand-me-downs from people in earlier times. Even though the tendency is to say our faith hinges on a hope and expectation that we will resurrect with our loved ones, I believe we need to place more value on our loved ones in this life and treasure their memories as endearing parts of our lives. These memories are useful in enhancing our own lives and the lives of our loved ones with whom we live. My ideas on these matters constitute the subject of this chapter. Bear with me as I delve into a very sensitive area of our faith.

The traditional idea that there is a place somewhere for us after we die becomes less and less important if we can accept another idea of eternity—that is, an experience of eternity now. At present, we are imperfect and oftentimes burdened with sickness and wants that never seem to end. It is very understandable to wish, at the end of our lives, for good riddance to these imperfections and wants and to finally be taken up into another world, as we have been taught since childhood. There is comfort in thinking a heavenly existence waits for those who expect it to come. We would like to say goodbye to this earthly condition and welcome the glorified presence of a postmortal existence. I think these beliefs are distracting us from our present spiritual journey. We need to look at the resurrection of Jesus as it relates to a personal experience about our own eternity in the here and now. I would like to expand on an idea derived from some traditional mystics recognized by the church.

Mystics in Church History

There have been numerous mystics in church history who have talked about an eternity in the here and now but not necessarily as opposed to the *pie in the sky when you die* belief. However, their vision of eternity in the here and now was very general, since most mystics in the past maintained a strong belief in the hereafter.

However, there were many who labored for the good of others as if this kind of activity were the most important call in their lives, not a life in the hereafter. I have selected just a few who in some way exhibited this vision. They are St. Gregory of Nyssa in the fourth century, St. Gregory the Great in the late sixth century, St. Teresa of Avila in the sixteenth century, and finally Thomas Merton in the twentieth century. I would like to share some interesting stories about these four dedicated religious persons.

St. Gregory of Nyssa was a very humble bishop who lived as a simple Cappadocian monk in Middle Eastern Europe. Although he used different words, he actually brought into focus the ideas behind the subtitle of my book (*Definition, Discovery, and Quest*) through his lectures and homilies. He preached that understanding God is a constant quest, because God is infinite, and humankind can never reach an understanding of God. There has to be a constant progression. The individual transcends all that has been revealed before. We reach an understanding of God not by knowledge but by meditation, an awareness that allows us to move ahead in the presence of God. He emphatically taught that the soul should rise above the senses and that true peace can only be found in the contempt of worldly pleasures. Many historical theologians consider him the founder of Christian mysticism. I believe he hinted at the possibility that total fulfillment in God can never be reached and (I add) eternity is found in this journey that never ends.[40]

St. Gregory the Great is a person of special interest for me because I consider him to be my patron saint. This Italian was the last of the four key doctors of the church. During the late sixth century, his life as both a pope and Benedictine monk exemplified a wonderful balance between prayer life and devotion to the rights of the poor. He balanced his efforts in trying to overcome the devastation brought on by the plague and the invasions of the kingdoms to the north, while maintaining a civil relationship with the Eastern Church. He is considered a mystic and practiced severe asceticism (fasting), which led to lifelong illnesses. The majority of his contemplation and theology focused on the importance of the sacraments. His contemplation led him to appreciate the sacraments (the Holy Eucharist, primarily), as a way of communicating and being in communion with the holiness of the eternal God. His prayer life became an experience of God. Although his ideas may be somewhat simple, he is considered to be the first authority in ascetical, moral, and mystical theology.

Many centuries later, we have St. Teresa of Avila and Thomas Merton. These mystics promoted a form of transcendental meditation, in which state the soul is uplifted from any form of materiality to a personal experience of bliss, or an experience of a deep communion with God.

St. Teresa of Avila, in the sixteenth century, was an amazing figure in Christian mysticism during the time of the Reformation. In her effort to reform her religious order, she pursued deep self-contemplation. Obsessed with rectifying abuses in religious life at the time, Teresa insisted on abject poverty and obedience throughout her newly reformed Carmelite order. Exercises in self-punishment were used to purify any material desires or sinfulness. She promoted devotions of silence, which culminated in experiencing a form of ecstasy. This form of perfect union with God was her experience of the eternal presence of Christ. It was through self-inflicted pain and suffering that she experienced eternity. Her understanding of eternity required her to rise above any material desires and the goods of the earth. (For more information on St. Teresa's life, please refer to my endnotes.[41])

The interesting observation about these early saints is the insistence on self-punishment and deprivation of materials things. It was not a question of using the goods of the earth for good purposes. It was more or less doing without material things for achieving a sense of the eternal. Admittedly, I do not relate very well to the total deprivation of the goods of this earth, but I do see what the goal was in their austere ways of life. It was their way of experiencing eternity in the here and now.

Thomas Merton's life (1915–1968) embodied a constant struggle with his understanding of the meaning of human life. He was attracted to the values and contributions of Hinduism and Native American spirituality. The injustices found in modern society could have acted as both a distraction and attraction to his contemplative life as a Trappist monk. Even today, his legacy is considered visionary, attempting to unify spirituality (eternal values) with the values of the world. However, as I see it, the experience of eternity for Merton and most mystics limited them to a meditative realm in their prayer life that required an out-of-the-world experience to be in communion with God. Thomas Merton's idea of eternity, although noble, is not exactly the idea of eternity I would like to propose.

The early mystics should be honored for what they were: truly devoted to God and a constant source of inspiration for anyone seeking self-fulfillment. The examples I have shared with you convey an understanding of eternity and how they experienced a timeless and immaterial state. However, the views of these visionaries are different from what I am speaking of when I treat the eternal. In my proposal, a grasp of the eternal requires that eternity be grounded in this world, not another world. Furthermore, I move away from the idea that mystical presence requires self-infliction of pain and punishment. Deprivation of the necessities of life ends up in fruitless hallucinations and cannot be a lifelong model for me.

Eternity as Experienced through the Kingdom of God

As much as I would like to think of eternity as something to be understood through a rational process, it is more of a deep quiet mindfulness of God by continually living in his divine presence. The idea of eternity is both incredible and incomprehensible without the whole body-mind process connected to an act of faith. Much like love, our faith embodies our human person. I suggest, as part of our faith act, we consider eternity as an experience of the kingdom of God here on earth and the resurrection of Christ within us now. This is where our faith should be focused. Far from being incredible, the kingdom of God is now real, based on the experience we have with the good news Jesus brought from His Father.

We need to look at eternity the way we have looked at the kingdom of God in our hearts. His kingdom is a forever experience of the good news of the Father being fulfilled in our lives. This is not just an experience of being lost in a deep meditation about what lies ahead when we die but can be an eternal experience right now.

I think eternity and the kingdom of God were two distinct concepts for the early Christians. Asked by the Pharisees when the kingdom of God was to come, Jesus gave them this answer, "The kingdom of God does not come in such a way as to be seen. No one will say, 'Look here it is!' or 'There it is!'; because the kingdom of God is within you."[42]

In other words, if you are to experience eternity, you must know that you need to experience Jesus and His good news in the here and now. Then, in turn, you become Jesus and the kingdom of God (eternity) for others. The rest of the episode in St. Luke's Gospel carries the idea of a postresurrection community trying to understand the supposed coming of Jesus and the end of the world. Could it be that the kingdom of God and eternity are different sides of the same coin? I think so.

My faith tells me that Jesus is teaching an altogether different idea of eternity from the Pharisees' understanding of God's restoration of the kingdom of Israel. For most Jews at the time of Jesus, eternity was an amorphous idea resulting from the belief that Israel would once again be established in a physical place (Jerusalem) with all the trappings of the former dynasty of King David. The kingdom of God necessarily embodied a material presence of God, with power over all kingdoms. However, Jesus was quick to correct this false assumption by saying that His kingdom resides in the hearts of believers and is not an external place where believers live forever.

Jesus did a lot of praying in His life, much to the wonder and puzzlement of His disciples, but His prayer, as I see it, was to reconnect with His own humanity and all that it meant to Him at that time. His idea of prayer is not exactly like the prayer of the ancient mystics, as documented in their teachings. In our Christian tradition, we have always held close the importance of the resurrection narratives as described by the Gospel writers. Not only did our Savior Jesus Christ suffer and die, but He also rose from the dead. This story about the resurrection is of paramount importance in the letters of St. Paul to the Romans, where St. Paul says that if Jesus did not rise again from the dead, our faith is in vain.[43] Without denying the authenticity of this belief, it is still possible to look at the resurrection into eternity in another way.

Another Look at Jesus's Resurrection

Jesus spoke of the kingdom of God existing in the minds and hearts of Christian believers. I ask now, is there possibly a new understanding of the resurrection, if these words of Jesus are true? I believe we can say that every time we practice the good news of Jesus Christ, we are allowing Jesus's resurrection to take place, putting into the present something about which Jesus spoke many times, though his disciples still did not understand it. In other words, Jesus rises up from the dead each time we visit the sick, help the needy, and perform a host of other actions that are characteristic of the kingdom of God.

It is not that we have discarded the traditional idea of the resurrection of Jesus. It is just that in terms of today's world, we can experience what eternity is like now. We can verify in our hearts and minds our own resurrection when we see Jesus in the sick, the downtrodden, and those in need of our help. Eternity as a *place where* becomes less important in our quest for fulfillment. Gerard Manley Hopkins, a great Jesuit poet in the early twentieth century, spoke of the resurrection of Jesus. This is an excerpt from "Kingfishers Catch Fire."

> Each mortal thing does one thing and the same:
> Deals out that being indoors each one dwells;
> Selves—goes itself; *myself* it speaks and spells,
> Crying What I do is me; for that I came.
> I say more: the just man justices;
> Keeps grace: that keeps all his goings graces;
> Acts in God's eye what in God's eye he is—
> Christ—for Christ plays in ten thousand places,
> Lovely in limbs, and lovely in eyes not his
> To the Father through the features of men's faces.[44]

Of all the great poetry in the world, there is none that has affected my thinking more about the purpose of a Christian life than Hopkins's poem, "Kingfishers Catch Fire." Each of the lines reflects his belief in an eternal purpose to his life. Each mortal being exhibits what dwells inside itself, but being just is what keeps his life eternal and graceful and empowers him to be the resurrected Christ, as Christ moves around in our present times.

Resurrection and eternity can be welded into one and the same thing—the imitation of Jesus. Our Savior's kingdom is what justifies our good actions. This is Jesus, who rose from the dead, Jesus who is constantly and eternally being resurrected in us now, not just one time in the past. We should never discard the *what* in biblical history, nor the traditional understandings of resurrection and eternity as if they were irrelevant. They offered solace and comfort to the disciples during those turbulent times and will continue to do the same for ages to come. However, there is much more that can be gleaned from traditional stories if we view them as an invitation to look at the meaning of the words *resurrection*, *eternity*, and *the kingdom of God* in a new way. The difference is realizing that these terms relate to something more than what was understood in the past. The kingdom of God is constantly coming, the resurrection is constantly happening, and eternity can always be here and now.

What would our attitude be if the traditional idea of eternity did not exist? Then I believe we would, as Christians, treasure every moment of time we have here on this earth. Living the kingdom of God as Jesus speaks of it would have amazing consequences for helping us understand our quest for fulfillment. Fulfillment is here in our space-time-dimensions. As I have mentioned many times, the important thing about fulfillment is that it is incomplete and must always involve a search. Just as evolution is the driver for change in our biological world,[45] so also our quest for fulfillment becomes the catalyst for forming new insights into God and eternity.

By bringing spirituality and evolution together, we can experience a continual movement forward, which brings satisfaction to our minds and hearts. Once we accept this phenomenon as a key element in life, we can see how we must always move ahead with our spiritual lives and work with this life as the most important part of our existence. This excludes the *pie in the sky* belief when we die. I believe looking ahead to another form of glorified existence, as in a place called heaven, is not how the kingdom of God works.

The kingdom of God is always coming and needs to be experienced now. Traditional thinking about the resurrection, the kingdom of God, and eternity will not stand the test of time. Jesus is here. Jesus has and is resurrecting as we speak. What is important is the here and now of eternity. Consequently, what has been declared as fact in the past becomes less and less important for us because eternity is already here. Although not specifically spelled out, the creation wheel proposal in chapter 4 implies that eternity is here and now as we move ahead in space and time.

I am not denying Jesus's resurrection in the past. My point is that we need to look at what resurrection could mean for us now, not what it meant to the disciples of Christ three days after He was nailed to a cross. What we know from our faith about eternity is adapted from early Christian tradition. That early Christian tradition held a deep conviction that Jesus would come back to take every believer to that other place called the kingdom of God. That did not happen, so a new idea about eternity being *somewhere* arose to comfort those who longed for the resurrected Jesus in their lives. It was not just a poem that Hopkins wrote as he faced death from typhoid fever. He was sharing an insight into how we can experience the resurrected Jesus as he rises up through our own good actions (justices). The resurrection and eternity are occurring all the time. Each day of our lives can be an experience of eternity in the kingdom of the Father.

A Life with Loved Ones after Death

This view of eternity brings up another point. Most of us experience a longing to be with our deceased loved ones after we die. But the longing to see our loved ones can only be fortified by a faith that we ourselves will not altogether die and disappear. Although this faith tradition we treasure in our heart is valuable, it does not help us move ahead with potentially new discoveries about eternity. If there is not an *out there* with glorified bodies, occupying a glorified place (heaven), then how will the power of faith fill this apparent void brought on by not seeing our loved ones again? How will this affect our daily lives? What difference will this make in the here and now? These are very good questions, and a new faith formation is needed to cope with these challenges arising from a new understanding of eternity. I cannot give answers to this problem, only an invitation to think in a different way about what happens at the end of our lives.

Death is very real and punishing for those of us who are left behind. Most of us experience a rupture and loss when a loved one dies. It is true, a sense of loss and grief are important for a healing process to begin. However, we cannot continue to live in the past. Elizabeth Ammons provides us with a beautiful way of managing our feeling about the loss of a loved one.

> You can shed tears because they are gone, or you can smile because they lived. You can close your eyes and pray they will come back, or you can open your eyes and see all that they left for you. Your heart can be empty because you can't see them, or you can be full

of the love you shared. You can turn your back on tomorrow and live yesterday, or you can be happy for tomorrow because of yesterday. You can remember only that they are gone, or you can cherish their memory and let it live on. You can cry and close your mind and feel empty, or you can do what they would want. Smile, Open your heart, Love and go on.[46]

Etched in our psyche is the need to say to our dying loved ones that we will be with them in heaven someday. We do not have to forgo this form of tribute to our loved ones, but we should make this testament as an act of faith in some kind of fulfillment that is not evident now, but an expectation that will be eternalized in our lives. The concept of the eternal should be based in the present, with the kingdom of God being the eternal quest, not a place somewhere in the future. How does one convey this to a dying loved one? It is my belief that when we need to use words, we should always use words that are comforting to the one who is near death, whatever those words might be.

The belief that we will see our deceased loved ones and enjoy their presence again is supported by the belief in eternity being in a special place. I believe this *place where* is not related to what Jesus was preaching about when He spoke of the kingdom of God being within us. How did we get this *place where* belief if Jesus did not share it with His disciples? I do not know, but I have an idea.

St. John's Gospel (John 14) has Jesus telling His disciples at the Last Supper that where He is going, His loved ones will come as well. The kingdom of God and eternity as being *somewhere* were also preached by St. Paul and members of the early believing community as connected to their belief in the impending end of the world and the last judgment. However, the end of the world and the last judgment did not arrive. Jesus did not come back again. Furthermore, the early Christians were suffering dire persecution for their beliefs and practices, and they asked where Jesus was. Jesus's prophetic messages in St. John's Gospel were not coming true, and St. Paul's statements about being prepared for the last judgment did not hold up.

Although the early Christians preached that Jesus was going to come again soon, He did not come back, and the world did not end with the destruction of Jerusalem. As a result, the ideas of the imminent end of the world, the last judgment, and eternity necessarily took a new turn and evolved into ideas of last judgment and eternity being unforeseeable future events. The belief about the kingdom of God and eternity as a *place where* and in the future holds firm even to this day.

Just before the birth of Christ, the classical Roman poet Horace voiced his idea of eternity. He said, "Non omnis moriar" (I will not altogether die),[47] which meant for many that there must be a place for us after death, and, therefore, there will necessarily be others with us. But Horace had no such idea in mind, as he was an atheistic hedonist. He was probably referring to the lasting value of his poetry, not to life after death. But for us as Christians, importance is not in things or accomplishments but rather in lasting happiness.

The concept of happiness enters in (as discussed in chapter 2) as a form of spiritual contentment based on the belief that we begin to enjoy an experience about the love of life right now, not sometime far away in a place where the kingdom of God is located. During our lives, I think we need to admit that the traditional idea of eternity is based on a distinct belief initiated in ancient times. As we move ahead with new insights about the life hereafter, the traditional concepts will fall short in offering a sense of assurance and confidence to the modern believer.

My proposal about the love of life being the basis of a true spiritual happiness is not new. In different words and scenarios, we can find this theme in the writings of mystics, theologians, and philosophers of long ago. The difference here is that I see no value in asserting that the kingdom of God is somewhere else, nor that the hereafter is more important than our quest for fulfillment in this life. The journey through this life has to be more important than arriving at the hereafter.

What Others Think about Life Now versus Life after Death

At this time, I would like to direct you to people who speak of the love of life in the present as being the most important feature of life. The first quotation is from Dale Carnegie:

> One of the most tragic things I know about human nature is that all of us tend to put off living. We are all dreaming of the same magical rose garden over the horizon, instead of enjoying the roses that are blooming outside our windows today.[48]

What Mr. Carnegie is saying does not contradict an afterlife. But he does say that we have to go outside ourselves and smell the roses in order to appreciate the real eternal values that life affords us in the present. It is a very insightful statement—that in order to appreciate eternity, we need to appreciate the events and experiences in life now.

The second quote comes from Joseph Campbell, and he is very blunt about the subject:

Eternity isn't some later time. Eternity is that dimension of the here and now, which thinking in time cuts out. This is it. And if you don't get it here, you won't get it anywhere. And the experience of eternity right here and now is the function of life.[49]

Mr. Campbell's statement should not be taken lightly. We know nothing in fact about the afterlife, but we do know about the here and now. We are sensual beings, and we should work and live as if there is nothing in the beyond. It is only in a faith act that we can even imagine anything else. Campbell goes on to say something very insightful:

If the path before you is clear, you're probably on someone else's.[50]

Since, in faith, we are truly on a journey to an ever-more-fulfilling God experience, the path is not and cannot be clear but only vague at best. If you see clearly the path to fulfillment in your life, you are probably walking on someone else's previously marked-out path or idea of what eternity is all about.

The following two quotes specify a common directive that we should treasure what we have now, because this is all there is. Mind you, we simply do not know, verifiably speaking, about any kind of life after death. However, the fact that we do not know a thing for sure does not deny its reality. This is where our faith comes into play. Nonetheless, these quotes are a good reminder that we must never lose sight of living in the present, instead of living for something in a future life. The first one is from Dan Buettner:

> I wake up in the morning and I see that flower, with its dew on its petal, and the way it's folding out, and it makes me happy, she said. It's important to focus on the things in the here and now, I think. In a month the flower will be shriveled and you will miss its beauty if you don't make the effort to do it now (appreciate it now). Your life, eventually, is the same way.[51]

The second one is from Nhat Hanh:

> Sometimes we believe that happiness is not possible in the here and now, and that we need a few more conditions to be happy. So we run toward the future to get the conditions we think we are missing. But, by doing so, we sacrifice the present moment; we sacrifice true life.[52]

In traditional Christian thinking, we are told that we should live for a future life, but I believe that it is important to go beyond this kind of thinking. We have to make use of this life as it is now, as if this life is all that there is. We need to look at the here and now as most important and work as if there were nothing else to look forward to after we pass away. My point is that our faith should engender a sense of eternity right now and in the present time. Our faith carries us through death as a new beginning, about which we know nothing. We need to bring the concept of eternity into the present, not something that begins after we take our last breath. Mario de Andrade, famous poet from Brazil, concludes my quotations about the importance of life in the here and now.

We have two lives and the second begins when you realize you have only one.[53]

My treatment of the hereafter should not take away valuable traditional beliefs about heaven and the hereafter, with or without loved ones. What it does is put a special perspective on the matter of eternity. Facts of faith really are not facts, and eternity is just one component of our faith, a virtue that always carries the elements of trust and hope. However, an experience of the kingdom of God can only come from living out the here and now, in the presence of Jesus, His Word, His good news.

From the beginning of this chapter, I felt it important to delve into my sincere belief that a new understanding of eternity is possible, without looking at a place to find God, and what that place may be in terms of fulfillment. Furthermore, I attempted to look at a new way of experiencing the eternal now. Lastly, I felt it important to show that what Jesus taught in His parables could be directly related to His new insight about the kingdom of the Father being here on earth. As believers, the only way we can enjoy the kingdom of God is to be Jesus for other people.

For many, this new insight into what Jesus taught may be unacceptable, because it goes against the traditional and treasured beliefs of the past. However, what I have proposed is a new look at an old teaching in the church. After starting by defining heaven as a place where, we travel in our minds and hearts long distances, only to arrive at the same idea, heaven, but a heaven as being in our hearts. We see heaven as something quite different yet credible. With the discovery of eternity being the kingdom of God here and now, we continue our quest and realize the journey to fulfillment is the eternity worth talking about.

We do not discard any definitions given to us in the past. We discover something new about what we have been taught. We live in a space-time continuum, not an eternal and resurrected life envisioned by saints of the past. Furthermore, Jesus has been and will continue to resurrect in us now. In a sense, we can say our eternity is the journey or quest for fulfillment. No one will find total fulfillment in this space-time continuum.

Once again, there is no such thing as a traditional idea of eternity in our worldly experience. We can only imagine it with the eyes of faith. We do have faith-powered dreams about heaven, but these cannot form any kind of fulfillment for us, only a conviction that we will somehow live eternally. I think my idea of eternity is credible, but it requires an act of faith. We can only fantasize what heaven might be like, but we can begin to enjoy the risen Christ now. I think Jesus is trying to tell us that we need to quit looking up in the skies for an answer and look into our hearts for the eternal kingdom of God. When we reflect the personality of Jesus in our actions to others, we begin to experience how this kingdom of God on earth is truly eternal, and nothing else really matters.

13

Can We Find Eternal Meaning in Life? It Is Time to Start Looking.

The intent of this final chapter is to explore how finding meaning in our lives is associated with a quest for fulfillment. Searching for and finding meaning for me has been much like a quest for fulfillment, in that the object of the quest is a goal always a bit beyond my reach. In other words, God is always a bit beyond my grasp.

To experience happiness or contentment as associated with a belief in God requires another look at our raison d'être and living our lives in the fullest possible way. To achieve this meaning in life assumes a purpose lived out in the present, not in the future or after death. I believe meaning or purpose in our lives now is crucial for happiness and fulfillment. In turn, when we achieve an understanding of what meaning or purpose is in our lives, then we can experience what happiness is at any given time. Happiness enters in as a by-product or side effect of finding the meaningfulness we want to achieve.

Primary Purpose in Life

At this time, I feel it important to relate our discussion on eternity to what a Christian calls their primary purpose for living. Since we are encased within a space-time framework in our existence, we have absolutely no idea of what eternity might be, let alone an eternal meaning in our lives. Anyone who says that eternity is a place where there is no end can only speak from a construct formed within the mind. It could easily be said that eternity has no beginning as well. But we have no idea how there can be no beginnings and no endings to existence. So also, eternal happiness is a construct of the mind and nothing else. To take the word or promise of a person of authority on the matter represents a terrific leap into the unknown. We really have no idea what *forever*, *eternity*, and *eternal happiness* mean. It will always be a manner of speaking. Now I ask, how does eternal (ultimate) meaning fit into a Christian view of life? We should at least be able to talk about it!

Not all is lost. When thinking about spiritual matters involving our quest and search for God in our lives, we will always come across something that stops us in our tracks. But we should remember that not only do we find that our continual quest for God gives us strength and purpose, but it offers a sense of contentment and fullness of spirit as well.

We can say that this experience (quest) is eternal in nature, in that this quest will give us a sense of an eternal meaning. This experience is crucial because it brings our hope in the future into the present. Being on a quest brings a sense of eternity to the present, not just wishful thinking that I will have my pie in the sky after death. It is not that the common understanding of eternity must be removed from our traditional deck of cards. It is to say that what we mean by eternity can take on a different and richer meaning for us now. Once again, I say that through a continual search for ultimate fulfilment, we can experience a deep and meaningful understanding of eternity in our lives right now.

May I use the example of a love experience? Although love takes on a variety of meanings, similar to a piece of cloth that shows a variety of shades of color, we can still grasp what love is and how we need to continue that experience in our lives. A God experience takes on many different meanings and becomes an ever-richer experience as we become more sensitive and mature in understanding our search for God. It is as if each step in our quest for fulfilment provides us with a new and satisfying shade and texture to the meaning of eternity.

Continuing with the example of love, the desire to love, be loved, and to bathe in that experience becomes a very powerful force or strength. Humankind always needs to nurture this experience of love if meaningfulness in our existence is to occur. In the same way, we can say that meaningfulness, as in the purpose of love, becomes ever more fulfilling, putting our own *reason for being* into the life we are presently experiencing. This allows us to manage any challenge or obstacle to a specific goal, particularly when that goal is an ongoing sense of happiness and fulfillment.

The Legacy of Victor Frankl

I wish to use the life of a well-known neuropsychiatrist, Victor Frankl (1905–1997), to illustrate my ideas about finding ultimate purpose, meaning, and fulfilment in our lives. A quest for meaning resulted in Frankl's work, *Man's Search for Meaning*. A prisoner during the Holocaust, Frankl survived horrific conditions, including starvation, torture, and inhumane treatment in the concentration camp at Auschwitz. Of dire importance was subsistence. It was paramount during his imprisonment that he stay alive and make it through his ordeal, as he believed that the punishment would not last forever.

Being a neuropsychiatrist, with a strong mind and determination, he understood that there had to be a purpose that drove him on and gave meaning to everything he had to undergo to stay alive. There were three principles that helped him endure. They were purposeful work, love, and courage in the face of difficulty. Being strong of heart and body, he was able to fabricate some sort of sense out of the make-work details he and his fellow prisoners faced. His love for his wife became an important force, which lifted him up and carried him through the insanity that existed in a very dark environment. Later on, after his release at the end of World War II, he found his wife had already died in a distant prison camp. However, the thoughts he had developed from his ordeal carried on to become a significant theme, permeating all of his teachings and accomplishments in psychotherapy. Ms. Maria Popova accurately described some highlights of Frankl's teaching moments:

> As a professor of neurology and psychiatry at the University of Vienna Medical School, Frankl's many lectures were always clear with his pedagogy that "the most important factor for keeping your sanity was to firmly hold on to some future goal, and take possession of your inner mind. Live as if you were living already in a second time, and as if you had acted the first time as wrongly as you are about to act now." He often tied his method of survival in the prison camp into the realm of an ultimate purpose in life. Without referring to the existence of God, he would say the following: "Listen for a victorious 'yes' in answer to my question of the existence of an ultimate purpose." Being insulted, he communed with his beloved wife. Her presence became more and more felt. "Don't aim at success—the more you aim at it and make it a

target, the more you are going to miss it. For success like happiness, cannot be pursued. It must ensue, and it only does so as the unintended side effect of one's dedication to a cause greater than oneself."[54]

In my earlier days, when teaching Philosophy of Religion to my high school students, I found Frankl's well-known book to be a great introduction to the importance of looking for true meaning and purpose in their lives. Although the concept of God was probably not Frankl's ultimate intent, such methodology became for me, as an instructor, a terrific segue into the possibility of God being an ultimate purpose for deep happiness in one's life. As I look back, I should have used the concept of ultimate purpose as a quest for ultimate meaning as well.

When discussing the topic with the students, it did not occur to me that searching for ultimate meaning really meant that one would never possess the ultimate meaning that is God. Frankl implied that success in all ventures in life, even spiritual, was only experienced as a by-product and that a drive for ultimate meaning had to continue in one's life as an ongoing search. Nonetheless, I was hopeful that some students would make a connection with a spiritual value here. With some thought on the matter, perhaps the students would leave themselves open to the experience of God and eventually discover that the quest was the important drive, not the possession of anyone else's idea about God.

A Closer Look at Humankind's Search for Ultimate Meaning

Victor Frankl produced many works, and his lectures were numerous. Of importance to me was his first book, as explained above, as well as a much later work, *Man's Search for Ultimate Meaning*. In this latter work, he made it clear that his discipline of logotherapy had the sole purpose of bringing about personal healing and well-being. Logotherapy is a way of helping people to be responsible for fulfilling meaning in their lives.[55] He felt society was rampant with the idea that needs and wealth were the primary considerations for finding meaningfulness in life. Frankl insisted they are means to an end and are a cause of the great emptiness that many people experience today. An existential vacuum forms as society tries to fill man's search for meaning with "needs." Society fails to satisfy any need to find meaning in ourselves with the offer of gifts.[56]

Frankl's goal in his profession was to assist patients who were in despair, had suffered severe trauma, or were experiencing severe grief due to the loss of a loved one. For him, meaning in life (the goal for his patients) cannot be given; it must be found in the person.[57] As mentioned previously, there are three ways real meaning in life can be attained. The first is found in work—that is, participating in achieving something greater than oneself; the second is communicating and developing relationships with someone (love); the third is facing a challenge that we personally cannot change.[58]

When it comes to finding ultimate meaning in our life, Frankl offers some helpful insights. He distinguishes psychiatry and religion as two different disciplines, though there may be an overlapping at times (e.g., a religious psychiatrist). But in its true form, psychiatry is not interested in God as a source for finding ultimate meaning. Frankl was insistent that life is not dependent on our being religious or irreligious. A belief in a god can only serve as an explanation for different attitudes toward life and death.[59] Research in psychology indicated that those who have purpose and meaning in life tend to fear death less. Those who reported less purpose and meaning in their lives showed a higher fear of death.[60]

On another note, Frankl wholeheartedly agreed that to consider anything to be infinite is incomprehensible. Man is a finite being and has no idea of what infinite means. He believed we should remove the idea of monotheism and move the idea to one of humankind (focusing on the idea of the universality of humankind). This is done by finding ultimate meaning in oneself, not in a god somewhere. He does admit that logotherapy is not perfect, will always evolve, and should also "be open to religion."[61]

Lastly, Frankl believed in our search for ultimate meaning, though such a subject is necessarily beyond understanding:

> Specifically, I see the meaning of logotherapy in helping others to see meaning in life. But one cannot "give" meaning to the life of others. And if this is true of meaning per *se*, how much more does it hold for ultimate meaning? *The more comprehensive the meaning, the less comprehensible it is.* Infinite meaning is necessarily beyond the comprehension of a finite being. Here is the point at which science gives up and wisdom takes over. Wisdom is knowledge plus: knowledge—and the knowledge of its own limits.[62]

I am deeply impressed with Frankl's thoughts on ultimate meaning. The idea of a god or the word *God* does not have to enter into the conversation about finding meaning in one's life. We can never grasp a notion of the infinite in our lives. However, we are always on that journey to total fulfillment. I believe we can experience the divine presence as the quality of wisdom that goes beyond the knowledge of science. Our goal is to experience something in our lives that cannot and will never be entirely defined. This would of course fall in line with Frankl's ultimate search for meaning.

Once again, as we have discussed in prior chapters, the discovery of God is not a finality but rather an ongoing experience of divine presence. Eternity does not mean we will possess God as an ultimate meaning to hold onto but rather as an ongoing journey. We never understand God as the end of a pursuit; heaven is not a thing to be possessed, nor a location to be enjoyed as an eternal place. Living life to our fullest is the true meaning and purpose we can put into our quest for ultimate fulfillment in God.

These ideas and suggestions I have proposed will be hard for many to swallow, because we have that entrenched need and tendency to find finality in the same way we want to possess objects, and that is certainly not the case here. As we age, we see things much differently, because of the virtue we call wisdom. When we look at a spectacular landscape as beautiful, we are seeing the landscape again as if for the first time. There is no end to the beauty of a mountain landscape. It always demands another look. Well, the discovery of God is very much like a beautiful view. When we view it repeatedly, it will never look precisely the same. We will always find something we did not notice before. Viewing a discovery of God in our lives involves a constant quest, and this quest is what brings fulfillment in our lives—not a finished fulfillment but rather a journey never ending and never completed. We will never be able to put our proverbial suitcase down inside the doorway and say to ourselves that we have arrived at heaven. Eternity for the discoverer is in the here and now, and we need to move on, into what is meant as our ultimate fulfillment, God. Ultimate meaning is in the here and now.

The search for a God in our lives always involves a quest for fulfillment, not in eternity but in the present. Furthermore, our search for God will always be a quest of some sort. That quest should not lead us to frustration but rather into a new discovery and fulfillment. All we really need to do is to proverbially sit back and enjoy the journey, because that is what a deepening spiritual life should be all about. This is how I understand Victor Frankl's ultimate meaning from a Christian point of view.

A Final Note

As you have probably noticed, the pages of this book are much like pages in my life. There are passages in some of the chapters that indicate frustration with religious institutional structures having a tie-down effect on my life. But there are chapters that are invitational and enlightening, and the ideas within make me really happy to share with you. The important thing to remember is that I have always and still do treasure all of the traditional teachings about God and ultimate meaning in my life. However, it was my duty to move on through spiritual obstacles into new insights. This is what keeps my faith truly alive. If I had stopped looking at the landscape of my spiritual life, I would have developed an apathetic and static stance with my faith in God.

Having a background in theology, philosophy, and science, I felt it necessary to be somewhat critical about certain doctrines and dogmas imposed and mandated. I do accept all the traditional teachings, but I accept them for what they are, not for what I have been told they are. I find it distasteful to be told to believe everything given to me as true in the literal sense of the term. Just as I have grown and matured in my life span of more than eighty years, so also has my understanding and appreciation grown and matured.

The story of my spiritual life and development should not stop with the final pages of this book. My quest for self-fulfillment still goes on. My intent in this book was to provoke some thinking on important values and issues that you possess about your own faith. All Christians have and work within a framework given to them since they began to speak. I have called that framework of beliefs our initial definitions. The examples of the initial proposal were many, but the most important of all was that there is a God who is all-powerful, all knowing, and all benevolent. The other concepts (definitions) passed on are not as crucial but are still with us and need to be more fully discovered as well.

In the chapters of my book, my intent was to encourage you to continually search, not somewhere else but somewhere within yourself. Each chapter is meant to show that, if faith were truly alive and vibrant, it would always be questioning (questing) for more insight into a faith experience. It is important to evaluate if hand-me-downs from our religious tradition represent the final word about our beliefs. Those kinds of beliefs will never outlast the test of our journey in faith, or even the test of time. The deeper meanings behind our faith definitions will always need to be rediscovered, evaluated, and lead us into a further quest for answers and values in our faith experience.

There are many insights that have become the defining moments of our faith in our lives. What is important is that these theological terms continually take on a deeper meaning as our faith matures. As I have often said in this book, we need to take a treasured belief and go all the way around the world of our faith and see that belief as if it were a brand-new discovery. With every new discovery we happen to come upon, the light of our faith should become a bit brighter. It is within our mind's new discovery of God that we give birth to another act of faith, resulting in a deeper faith experience. It is upon this insight that we are encouraged to nurture our faith in the future.

From our early years of wonder to the enlightening moments of our senior years, we continually give birth to experiences of wisdom. This special kind of birth in wisdom happens when we integrate our knowledge and experiences in life. As we age, we begin to find out what life is all about—that is, the purpose and ultimate meaning for being. I truly wish that in everyone's heart, there would be a place for the kingdom of God as a form of ultimate meaning. Incompletely grasped and unfulfilled as it might feel to be at times, the sense of the presence of God should still be there. The Holy Spirit has always been there in some form but needs to be felt in new and different ways.

The quest of which I have spoken many times is the crucial component of a faith process. The quest is like a journey that never ends, is never finished, and is never complete. This journey in faith is what I understand as eternity, always moving forward. In our world of space-time, our quest for fulfillment is about as close as we can get to understanding what eternity can mean for us as we journey through this life. This invitation is to see the journey in life as a true experience of eternity, and a continual invitation to expand our search for God in a different way. A continual quest for God has terrific potential for expanding our faith experience. The kingdom of God is here. Following the good news of Jesus Christ is how we bring to life the historical person of Christ and the kingdom of God. This is how Christ has resurrected for us and becomes eternal for us. When we accept each discovery, we can understand how eternity is continually being born in our lives.

Acknowledgments

Writing a book is not an easy task. In my case, the finished product required an endless amount of work. I wish to recognize special supporters of my insights for this book. In particular, I am indebted to my wife, Carol, who very patiently offered her expertise as a professional writer in the completion of each chapter. Her insistence on critical thinking for each idea helped me reach my goal of communicating clearly what I wanted to say.

Besides my wife, I am deeply grateful to my son, Michael, for his close examination of the manuscript. My thanks also go out to Harvey Loria, my English teacher colleague, who meticulously worked on the wording in each of the chapters.

Lastly, I must acknowledge that my insights in this book do not offer total satisfaction or answers to the many ideas contained within the cover. Giving answers was not my intent. As in my first book, the purpose was to offer a direction to the inquiring mind, not finished and static answers to any questions.

Throughout the chapters in my book, I urge the readers to evaluate what constitutes a drive for a closer relationship with our creator and the importance of continuing a personal quest for experiencing a divine presence in their lives.

In some way, we are all searching for a God in our lives, not necessarily a miracle worker but a presence that leads us to some kind of personal fulfillment and possibly an ultimate meaning.

Good luck to all and may the journey through life continue to offer an eternal experience.

Endnotes

Introduction

1   J. Gregory Steiner, *Evolution of Belief: A Christian Perspective for the Future* (Bloomington, IN: Archway Publishing, 2018).

Chapter 1

2   AZQuotes.com. Schuller actually obtained this quote from T. S. Eliot "The Gidding," *The Four Quartets*, 1943.

Chapter 2

3   Guru Mithreshiva, Quora.com.
4   Timothy Wilson, *Redirect* (New York: Little, Brown and Company, 2011), 52.
5   Ibid.
6   Goodreads.com/Work/Quotes/1427207 Confessions.
7   Anthony Padovano, *Dawn Without Darkness* (New York: The Missionary Society of St. Paul the Apostle, 1971), 23.
8   Gautama Buddha—500 BCE.

Chapter 3

9   Huffington Post.ca., *Adorable-Ways-Kids-Describe-God*.
10 Found in the psalms and alluded to as "Godliness," J. L. McKenzie, SJ, *Dictionary of the Bible* (Milwaukee: Bruce Publishing Company, 1965), 405.

Chapter 4

11 First used by Thomas Kuhn and defined by Merriam-Webster.com.
12 I refer the reader to Encyclopedia Britannica, vol. 2 of the Micropaedia, Ready Reference and Index, p. 1180, for an expanded reference; Also, *The Philosophy Book, Big Ideas Simply Explained*, 75.

Chapter 5

13 *Dictionary of Theology*, 409–413.

Chapter 6

14 The following are considered to be the five instances of the fall of man: the stories of Adam and Eve, Cain and Abel, Noah and the ark, the Tower of Babel, and Sodom and Gomorrah. They represent the judgment of God on the sins of man. Cf. McKenzie, *Dictionary of the Bible*, 827.
15 As referenced in *Evolution of Belief: A Christian Perspective for the future* (Bloomington, IN: Archway Publishing, 2018), xii.
16 *Kids Say the Darndest Things*, Kelly Wallace CNN, and *OMG, How Children see God*, CNN-CNN.com Dec. 23, 2015, and Crosswalk.com, Jan. 10, 2020.

Chapter 7

17 McKenzie, *Dictionary of the Bible*, 830.
18 Ibid., 314–316
19 Str.org.; bethinking.org; en.Wikipedia.org.

Chapter 8

20 Many doctrines, bulls (edicts), and practices of the Catholic Church indicate no salvation outside the church. Baptism is the accepted ritual for being saved. The Islamic religion mimics the centuries-long

practices found in the Old Testament for purifying disbelief in the one, holy, and all-knowing God. A vengeful God is the result of disbelief.
21 In the Pentateuch, elimination of the opposition was crucial for occupying the Promised Land. Safety, security, and protection of the chosen people meant that at least the opposing male warriors needed extermination.
22 McKenzie, *Dictionary of the Bible*, 136–137.
23 Catholicism.org/*Unbaptized infants*/Malone.

Chapter 9

24 Also submitted to Christianity.stackexchange.com on August 20, 2018.
25 McKenzie, *Dictionary of the Bible*, 251.
26 https:wwwcatholicculture.org/culture/librarydictionary/indexcfmpid=3657.
27 AZquotes.com/author.
28 Steiner, *Evolution of Belief*, 35.

Chapter 10

29 John 14:2, Jerusalem Bible, 140.
30 Exodus 20:10 ff; Numbers 10:33.
31 McKenzie, *Dictionary of the Bible*, 55.
32 Brainy Quotes.com.
33 Luke 17:21, John 3:5, Good News Translation, 833 and 843.

Chapter 11

34 34 AZquotes.
35 Calgary Herald, February 23, 2021.
36 Ibid.
37 Ibid.
38 Genesis 1:27.
39 *Calgary Herald*, February 25, 2021.

Chapter 12

40 Newadvent.org/cathen/07016a.htm; enwikipedia.org/wiki/gregory_of_nyssa.
41 Of note is that her fellow nuns spoke of periods of levitation and other paranormal experiences. She kept very meticulous records of her experiences, which led some later critics to think, correctly, that she was a victim of temporal lobe epileptic seizures and that her sisters were holding her in place rather than keeping her from levitating while at prayer. en.wikipedia.org/wiki Teresa of Avila.
42 Luke 17:21, Good News Translation, 833.
43 1 Corinthians 15:17.
44 "As Kingfishers Catch Fire," by Gerald Manley Hopkins, from *Poems and Prose* (New York: Penguin Classics, 1985).
45 Courtney Humphries, "Life's Beginnings," *Harvard* magazine, September 2013.
46 Lessonslearnedinlife.com
47 Horace's Ode 3.30.6, *The Ode on Immortality*.
48 Dale Carnegie (AZQuotes.com).
49 Joseph Campbell (AZQuotes.com).
50 Ibid.
51 Dan Buettner (AZQuotes.com).
52 Nhat Hanh (AZQuotes.com).
53 Cited from his poem, "My Soul Has a Hat," Poem Hunter.com.

Chapter 13

54 Maria Popova: www.Brainpickings.org.
55 Victor Frankl, *Man's Search for Ultimate Meaning* (New York: Basic Books, 2000), 119.
56 Ibid., 13.
57 Ibid., 112.
58 Ibid., 141.
59 Ibid., 125.
60 Ibid., 125.
61 Ibid., 13.
62 Ibid., 136.

Bibliography

Applewhite, E. J. *Paradise Mislaid*. New York: St. Martin's Press, 1991.

Az Quotes.com.

Buckingham, Will, Douglas Burnham, Clive Hill, Peter J. King, John Marenbon, and Marcus Weeks. *The Philosophy Book: Big Ideas Simply Explained*. New York: Dorling Kindersley, 2011.

Frankl, Victor. *Man's Search for Meaning*. Boston: Beacon Press, 2006.

Frankl, Victor. *Man's Search for Ultimate Meaning*. New York: Basic Books, 2000.

Funk and Wagnalls Standard Dictionary. New York: Funk and Wagnall, 1974.

Holy Bible: Good News Translation. New York: American Bible Society, 1992.

Jerusalem Bible: Reader's Edition. New York: Doubleday, 1968.

McKenzie, J. L., SJ. *Dictionary of the Bible*. Milwaukee: Bruce Publishing Company, 1965.

Padavano, Anthony. *Dawn without Darkness*. New York: Missionary Society of St. Paul the Apostle, 1971.

Rahner, Karl, and Herbert Vorgrimler. *Theological Dictionary*. New York: Herder and Herder, 1968.

Steiner, J. Gregory. *Evolution of Belief: A Christian Perspective for the Future*. Bloomington, IN: Archway Publishing, 2018.

Strong, James. *The Exhaustive Concordance of the Bible*. Peabody, Massachusetts: Hendrickson Publishers.

The Holy Qur'an. Translated by Maulawi sher 'Ali. Surry, UK: Islam International publications Ltd., 2011.

Webster's Encyclopedic Dictionary. New York: Lexicon Publications, 1988.

Wright, Robert. *The Evolution of God*. New York: Little Brown and Company, 2009.

CPSIA information can be obtained
at www.ICGtesting.com
Printed in the USA
LVHW040614170223
739433LV00001B/21

RELIGION - SPIRITUALITY

In Search of God invites you to enhance your faith

J. Gregory Steiner draws on his personal and r̶   e
to seek wisdom on the nature of God, divinit̶   d
eternity. He considers questions such as:

- How can Christians express new ideas withou̶   e
  believers?
- Does faith need to move in a new direction to attract people searching for God in their lives?
- Should our understanding of dogma and doctrine change as we grow into adulthood and beyond?

It is easy to discuss, on a philosophical and theological level, the need to change our ideas about creation, incarnation, and redemption in today's world. However, it is quite a challenge to deal with these needs from a kneeling position in a church pew.

Join the author as he explores how to navigate questions about religion and move the church forward.

J. Gregory Steiner, a former Jesuit for nineteen years, earned postgraduate degrees in biology and theology, and taught science and religion at the high school level. He lives in Calgary, Alberta, Canada. Having been retired for twenty-five years, he has focused his senior years on inviting Christians to re-examine outdated doctrines and dogmas of the Christian church in a new way. His first book, *Evolution of Belief* (2018), is a scientific analysis of the development of Christian belief over two thousand years.

U.S. $14.99

ARCHWAY PUBLISHING